RECENT REVOLUTIONS IN ANTHROPOLOGY

RECENT REVOLUTIONS IN ANTHROPOLOGY

Maxine P. Fisher

Blairsville High School Library

FRANKLIN WATTS 1986
NEW YORK   LONDON
TORONTO   SYDNEY
A SCIENCE IMPACT BOOK

Photographs courtesy of: Ed Lettau/Photo Researchers: p. 12 (top); Jules Bucher/
Photo Researchers: p. 12 (bottom); E. Boubat/Photo Researchers: p. 13; A.W.
Ambler from National Audubon Society/Photo Researchers: pp. 20, 36; Gordon S.
Smith from National Audubon Society/Photo Researchers: p. 21; Toni Angermayer/
Photo Researchers: pp. 24, 90; Dr. Georg Gerster/Photo Researchers: p. 26;
UPI/Bettmann Newsphotos: pp. 41, 59, 62; Susan Kuklin/Photo Researchers: p. 44;
K. Cannon-Bonventre/Anthro-Photo: p. 51; Camerapix/Photo Researchers: p. 56;
The New York Public Library Picture Collection: pp. 61, 98; AP/Wide World: p. 63;
#335796, American Museum of Natural History: p. 71; Tom McHugh, Field Museum
of Chicago/Photo Researchers: p. 73; Margo Crabtree: p. 75; #39685, American
Museum of Natural History/Photo Researchers: p. 76; Photo Researchers: p. 78;
Irven DeVore/Anthro-Photo: p. 84; Nancy Nicolson/Anthro-Photo: p. 88; Clem
Haagner/Photo Researchers: p. 89; F. B. Grunzweig/Photo Researchers: p. 91;
R. Feldman/Anthro-Photo: p. 101; Victor Englebert/Photo Researchers: p. 111;
Eugene Gordon/Photo Researchers: p. 113.

Library of Congress Cataloging-in-Publication Data

Fisher, Maxine P., 1948-
Recent revolutions in anthropology.

(A Science impact book)
Bibliography: p.
Includes index.
Summary: Examines the different areas of concern in
the field of anthropology and surveys recent theories
on such topics as sex roles, communication with
primates, and cultural change.
1. Anthropology—Juvenile literature.   [1. Anthropology]
I. Title.   II. Series.
GN3I.5.F57 1986   306   86-9223
ISBN 0-531-10240-8

CONTENTS

Blairsville High School Library

MANY GRATEFUL THANKS TO
FRANK SPENCER, KATHLEEN SISAK,
AND MICHAEL SPORN.

FOR STEVE

CHAPTER 1
WHAT IS
ANTHROPOLOGY?

A COMPLEX PROFESSION

If you were to pop in at an annual convention of morticians, most likely you'd hear about and see demonstrations of the latest techniques and tools of the mortuary trade. At a meeting of a national organization of computer salespeople, you'd expect to see and hear about the most recent developments in the machines and the marketing of them.

But go to the annual convention of the American Anthropological Association and put your ear to the doors as you wander from one to another of the vast conference rooms where more than twenty different discussions are simultaneously under way. At one you may hear mention of "morphemes that have parallel sets of allomorphs," at the next, talk of "amino acid racemization." One speaker is attempting to describe the inflection of verbs in the Shoshone Indian language, another a new technique for dating fossils. And so it continues along the corridor.

Unlike the meetings of other professional groups, those of anthropologists give the impression that the participants do not speak a common language, that what you are witnessing is more like a ritual ingathering of distantly related tribes whose babel is as confusing to one another as it is to the outside observer.

This is because when they are at work these people can be seen engaged in such different tasks as weighing the hundreds of pounds of sweet potatoes to be eaten at a big bash given by tribespeople in a remote part of New Guinea; climbing a fifty-foot tree in an Asian rain forest to tape-record the howls made by the long-limbed ape that lives there; examining under a microscope a *coprolite*—that is, a piece of excrement—left by someone in Illinois over a thousand years ago, perhaps as he or she was admiring a sunset or remembering a joke.

Is it possible that such different, and at first glance weird, kinds of activities have anything in common?

THE COMMON LANGUAGE

The answer is yes. Despite their very different tools, methods of research, and jargon, anthropologists are pilgrims in a single cause. They are all trying to fit pieces into the same puzzle. The puzzle will be complete when we know how our humanity was first achieved and then what made it go off in such different directions. In other words, why is it that in some ways populations behave quite similarly and in other ways quite differently? What accounts for the similarities? What accounts for the differences?

Take eating, for example. Like other organisms, we all need to eat in order to survive. But say that and you've almost exhausted what is universally true among us. There is much more to say about the differences we humans display in the ways we obtain, prepare, consume, and think about what we eat. Back in the first century B.C., the Roman philosopher Lucretius first observed that "one man's meat is another's poison." Anthropologists get much more excited by the idea that one *group's* meat is often another's poison.

Eating a Big Mac might be heaven for some of us, but quite likely it would be pure torture to a practicing orthodox Hindu, to whom the eating of beef is *taboo*, or strictly forbidden. On the other hand, most Americans (even those who boast that they will "eat anything") would feel a bit queasy about lunching on a small puppy, a Chinese gourmet delight of ancient and royal tradition.

And despite the differences in taste among them, members of all three groups would probably be equally horrified if while visiting a remote village in New Guinea they were served a plate of human brains. What we eat, like so much of our behavior, is closely linked with who we are and what we as members of a certain group think.

CULTURE

The number of ideas that we have in common with those around us—and which daily find their way into action—is really quite staggering. A complete list would include (among many others) our ideas about what is right and wrong, beautiful and ugly; those concerning food, work, lovemaking, courtship, marriage, divorce; what makes a good parent, son, daughter (and other relatives); and how to behave toward strangers, friends, animals, the earth, and finally the unseen forces at work behind them all.

Now think of a particular group of people. If you could take all of the ideas—and behaviors—they generally share as a result of being in more or less close contact, and then add their tools and technological know-how for dealing with their environment, you would have what anthropologists call the *culture* of these people. Culture, being shared, makes people feel part of a club. But neighboring clubs frequently have more or less the same ideas and rules. The differences among them often seem greater to their memberships than to outside observers.

Anthropologists often discuss the cultures of the world as if they were like the colors of the rainbow: each one unique at its center, yet blending at the edges with those nearby to form a spectrum that bedazzles the beholder. But we can no more draw the borders around a culture than grab hold of the rainbow. Culture isn't a thing; it, too, is an idea. What complicates things even further is that the cultures of some peoples are quite different from those of their neigh-

How many differences can you find
in the eating habits of the people
in these photographs? Above left:
An American family. Left: *A Moslem
family in Malaysia having dinner.*
Above: *An orthodox Hindu man, for
whom beef would be strictly taboo.*

bors. In these cases the cultures in question don't blend into one another but stand in sharp contrast to those surrounding them. They are less like a rainbow than a test pattern on a color TV.

However problematic, the idea of culture is a useful one. Anthropologists believe that by comparing and analyzing their descriptions of peoples around the world, they will eventually be able to explain many of the differences among us.

HUMAN NATURE

And now something should be said about "human nature." Almost everybody believes in it, but we still don't know, in a scientific sense, what it is. It's the reason people often give to justify essentially nasty behavior such as violence, greed, and male domination of women. The more cultures in which these behaviors are found, the more secure people feel in believing they are just part of human nature, tendencies programmed into our genes.

The problem is that culture is not only the *shared* behavior of a group. It is also the *learned* behavior of a group. You might think that just by living together in a group, individuals could learn from one another. But the connection between being around others and being able to learn from them isn't that simple.

An Italian honeybee, for example, can tell its hive mates exactly where to find a bonanza of honey it discovered while cruising about the countryside. It does this by performing an intricate kind of square dance in which the pattern of steps, tempo, and angle of the sun on its body combine to give a precise set of flight instructions. It's a feat of communication that seems as unbelievable as E.T. managing to "phone home," but it happens all the time.

But that Italian bee can't ever hope to communicate with Austrian bees, no matter how long it lives among them. The dance languages of the two groups are different, and the bees get their knowledge from their genes, not experience. We, on the other hand, can master a new language even when we begin studying it when we're well into maturity.

Joseph Conrad, the writer of English classic novels, didn't learn English until he was in his twenties. One day you might well write a famous book in French or Chinese or a computer language yet to be invented.

The point is that what makes us distinctive in the animal world is our stupendous capacity to learn. It is what has long enabled us to change with changing conditions. People who think that because aggression and greed are so widespread we must be doomed by our genes to have these qualities, are closing their eyes to what it means to be a learning species.

The question "what is human nature?" is central to those working in a new area called *sociobiology.* Sociobiologists take as their starting point the fact that humans are by far not the only social animal. They believe we must therefore look to the many other kinds of animals that live in groups for a comparative framework for understanding our behavior. If we look carefully, they say, we will discover that some behaviors are so widespread among social animals that they are as identifiable as organic structures such as lungs or fingernails or a tail.

What are these behaviors? Those pertaining to sex, as well as aggression, and altruism, the trait individuals display when they act solely for the welfare of others. According to sociobiologists, these and perhaps other behaviors are so pervasive among social animals that they must be controlled by a gene or complex of genes.

A significant proportion of human actions, they say, can be explained in the same way as the presence of biological organs is explained. That is, aggressiveness, for example, becomes a predominant trait in a population when it enables an individual—or his or her kin, since they share many genes—to leave behind relatively more offspring, who in turn are likely to pass the gene for aggression on to *their* offspring. In other words, some of our behavior has been subject to the same processes of evolution as our bodies.

What, you may well ask, is the evidence that a gene or complex of genes causes a specific type of behavior—such as the impulse to risk one's life in order to save one's children—to be transmitted down through the generations?

There is none. The science of genetics is at this time incapable of providing any such proof, though perhaps one day in the future it will be able to do so. For this reason, sociobiology is at the time of writing only a theory, and a hotly debated one at that.

But this is not to say that we have limitless freedom, that our biology places no constraints upon us. Nearly all normal people learn to walk on two legs, see the world in color and in three dimensions, and master a complex language quite easily at a very early age. These behaviors and others *are* the result of our evolution. The challenge is to sort out the real restraints from the real freedoms. This is exactly what anthropologists try to do. They ask: in what ways are we bound by our biology? In what ways are we free to be human, that is to say, a supremely *cultural* animal?

Their concern with the idea of culture, then, is the key that anthropologists hold in common. With it they hope to unlock a roomful of mysteries. With this in mind we can now get a more focused glimpse of these dauntless adventurers at work in the four subfields of American anthropology: physical anthropology, archeology, linguistics, and cultural anthropology.

CHAPTER 2
WHAT ANTHROPOLOGISTS DO

*W*hat exactly do the different kinds of anthropologists do? To answer the question in a general sort of way first, physical anthropologists are most concerned with human biology. They try to understand how it evolved in the course of millions of years, and how the process of change is continuing even today. Archeologists are interested in interpreting our more recent past, and mostly from the objects made by past peoples from around the world. Cultural anthropologists study living communities, not only for hints about human life in the distant past, but also to discover the similarities and differences among us. And as you might guess from their name, anthropological linguists look to language for their ideas about both past and living peoples.

WHAT PHYSICAL ANTHROPOLOGISTS DO

It's the physical anthropologists—whether in the laboratory or loose on the landscape—who most resemble a breed of Sherlock Holmses. Their mission is nothing less than to solve the mystery of how we came to be human. They ask: what chain of events led a tropical, tree-dwelling population of animals to evolve into two-legged creatures with a special power to learn and change?

The time range involved is roughly sixty million years; that is, if we count from the time when these tree-dwelling creatures began to develop some of the features they share with us humans. The critical evidence consists mainly of teeth, bone fragments, and skeletons excavated on three continents over the course of a century. No wonder the detectives spend much of their time debating and in investigating more accessible but less direct kinds of evidence.

PHYSICAL ANTHROPOLOGISTS AND PRIMATES

> D.J. was the striving executive type who had not yet reached the top. He was second in command, a rather frustrating position . . . for in such matters as determining the direction of travel and the time and duration of rest periods, the females and youngsters ignored him completely. He lay by himself on his back, one arm slung casually across his face, oblivious to the world.

> (Ollie) had this glassy expression and her behavior was quite aimless. She went off up a mountain and sat there, and came down again. . . . She had a vacant look in her eyes, an empty staring ahead—the same look that has been associated with grief in orphans.

D.J. was a wild gorilla, Ollie a chimpanzee mother stricken by the death of her infant. The descriptions of their behavior by George Schaller and Jane Goodall, respectively, two of anthropology's most celebrated fieldworkers, make these wild animals appear very human to us.* But even in the relative prisonlike setting of an old-fashioned zoo, gaze at any

*Schaller's description comes from his book *The Year of the Gorilla* (Chicago: University of Chicago Press, 1964), Goodall's from an interview entitled "Goodall and Chimpanzees at Yale" (*New York Times Magazine*, February 18, 1973).

monkey or ape long enough and it's almost impossible not to see "family" resemblances.

Take a look at the insect-eating tree shrew, the rat-sized tarsier, or a loris, which looks like it should be a Muppet, and it's another story. Yet all of them—monkeys, apes, tarsiers, and humans among others—constitute a single *order*, a category of beings seen by scientists to physically have more in common with one another than they do with other kinds of animals by virtue of their closer common ancestry.

The order is called *primates*, derived from the word meaning "of the first rank." We may be immodest in the scientific Latin names we assign to ourselves, but this term is a useful reminder. However tempted we may be to study wolves (or other animals whose behavior often seems quite humanlike) for clues to what made us human, it's our connection to the other primates that is of the first rank. It is their development physical anthropologists must come to grips with. Those who specialize in the study of these animals— our relatives—are called *primatologists.*

Even the alien-looking little tree shrew is important, because back in the days when great tracts of tropical rain forest began to cover much of the earth, its ancestor, a squirrel-size, ground-dwelling quadruped, took to the trees. That was about sixty million years ago and the move was probably due to the growing competition for food on the ground. But if these shrewlike creatures managed to avoid their competitors by taking to the trees, there was also a negative side to the course they had followed. Instead of having a secure foothold wherever they moved, as they were used to having, they encountered the constant hazard of tree-dwelling. Twigs suddenly broke under their weight, hurtling them downward, sometimes to their doom.

The need to move safely in the new environment favored the development of two features we share with all primates. The first was the possession of hands with flat nails instead of claws. The second was the ability to see in three dimensions. Called *stereoscopic vision,* this feature is the result of the eyes being placed at the front, rather than the sides, of the head. The abilities to snatch at branches with the hands and to see the tangle of the forest world with depth perspec-

Above: *the tarsier is the "jumping jack" of the primate order. (Note how long its legs are.) It is rare now, but 50 million years ago, many different varieties were to be found. Very much a "night owl" in its habits, the tarsier can also swivel its head 180 degrees.* Right: *a real-life Muppet. This loris from Southeast Asia moves about the trees with turtle speed. As you can see, its feet, like its hands, are well made for gripping. In fact, it will often hang from its feet while feeding and be able to hoist itself back onto a branch without using its hands. The earliest European observers of the loris named it from a Dutch word meaning "dopey," but we believe their ancestors also evolved into the very intelligent primates known as monkeys.*

tive were a boon to the early primates. In fact, without these abilities, such animals woudn't have gotten off the ground, evolutionarily speaking.

Some physical anthropologists argue that if the early primates had been strict vegetarians, their descendants would not be the animals we know. They say that the habit of grasping moving prey—mostly insects—was a major force in the development of a hand with separately moving fingers.

In any case, once they had moveable fingers, an improved vision center, and an enlarged skull to house it, the primates became beings "of the first rank." Far more numerous and varied than they are today, they became the masters of forests that stretched across three continents. In time their descendants would dominate the flatlands that eventually replaced much of the forest.

Physical anthropologists study the *fossils,* or organic remains, or once-living primates, including the extinct forms of creatures nearer to ourselves in time and appearance. With these they try to document the course by which particular organs, abilities, posture, behavior, and diet evolved and how they helped the primates in the trees (later on the ground) to beat the odds against their survival. *Paleoanthropologists* are those physical anthropologists whose study focuses on the time when humans were first emerging from the earlier primate stock.

Physical anthropologists don't rely entirely on bones to uncover the story of our emergence. They also study living animals. In the lab, some investigate the composition of blood chemistry for clues to our relationship to different primates in our family tree. Others meet the animals on their own turf to find out what behaviors we share with them.

Still others speculate on how the behavior of non-human primates might have shaped our own bodily needs and habits in ways that aren't at all obvious.

David Harsha is a physical anthropologist who thinks, for example, that the drop in our work efficiency during midafternoon—which can be measured by the increased frequency of job accidents during these hours—stems from the fact that as primates we've spent most of our recent evolutionary history in the tropics. According to Harsha and cultural anthropologist Marcia Thompson (see their article "Our Rhythms Still Follow the Tropical Sun" in the January 1984 *Psychology Today*), here is the evidence:

In most places not affected by the demands of heavy industry, people take much longer and later lunch breaks. Not only that. In such settings lunches tend to be animated by lots of socializing. Here the office worker who regularly forgoes the break and sits alone at a desk spooning down yogurt or wolfing down a sandwich, while continuing to answer the phone, would be regarded with pity and amazement. Throughout much of the world lunchtime is still viewed as something communal and sacred. At all costs it should not be interrupted by work or by strangers.

In the long, late, convivial lunch, people seem to be following patterns observed in troops of monkeys and apes. Unlike their carnivore neighbors, these animals do not use the midafternoon for catching a snooze, but for the rather important business of reaffirming their relationships to one another. How do they do this? Well, if you're a high-ranking chimp or adult baboon, it's the time for the exquisite pleasure of being groomed: sitting beside a subordinate troopmate while his or her fingers ripple through your fur and remove any bugs, dirt, or vegetation they come across.

Does it help to see the connection? Perhaps. Admittedly, few American workers would care to spend their afternoons in this manner. But if our primate need for a long, late very sociable lunch were to become the rule, the number of on-the-job accidents might decline considerably.

HUMAN VARIATION

Still other physical anthropologists study only living humans. They tend to measure the relatively small differences found among groups of people today: group differences in weight and stature, responses to metabolism tests, etc. Much of their work is aimed at trying to discover various patterns of human growth and development and adaptation in a wide range of environments.

"All in the golden afternoon." If you're
a baboon, the lunchtime break includes
the exquisite pleasure of being groomed.

WHAT ARCHEOLOGISTS DO

When I first announced to my family my decision to study anthropology, my father asked in amazement: "You're going to spend your life digging for pottery in the Yucatán?"

It's not an unusual response. For many people the term "anthropologist" conjures up the image of an archeologist. In that image archeologists are eternally digging. They are searching for old things, beautiful things, rare and wonderful treasure. However, few people know what these persistent seekers—as a group—think of their discoveries.

It is true that archeologists dig, for *archeology* is the study of prehistoric and historic cultures through the analysis of material remains, and often these remains lay buried beneath our feet. They include not only ruins of buildings and monuments, but also *artifacts*, objects made by people who often had no written language and therefore left no other record of their way of life. Tools, weapons, body ornaments, household furnishings, and items used in religious ceremonies are all examples of artifacts that typically turn up in excavations. But archeologists have always done more than just dig them up.

Like historians, they establish the sequence of events that occurred in a given place and time period. But unlike the historian, they take on a time span of roughly half a million years, and that includes the past century. Who needs archeologists, you may well ask, once we have written records? As archeologist James Deetz has pointed out, written history tells us the name of the Mayflower and much about what brought the colonists to Plymouth. But archeology is what teaches us what they ate when they got there.

Although this may seem far less important, it really isn't. What people eat, how they get it, and who controls its distribution are matters likely to influence everything else.

In fact, the big revolution in archeology these days is related to another great revolution, the one called the *Neolithic* era. That began almost ten thousand years ago, and it was essentially a food revolution. People in the Middle East and Mexico ceased to hunt and forage and fish for their meals and, as most of us do today, began to rely on those who took up food production as a full-time job. Without that

"Dig we must!" To the archeologist falls the job of
uncovering and analyzing the material remains of
cultures from the past. This site is in Nigeria, Africa.

change there would still be only small, technologically simple societies. The world as we know it, with movies and video and cars and the forty-hour workweek, simply would not exist.

Practitioners of what is called "the new archeology" try to do more than just piece together what happened in a particular time and place as gleaned from the artifacts excavated there. They try to fit those small, interlocking pieces into a bigger picture.

In particular, they want to document how—at different times and in different regions of the world—the big change took place in the way people exploited their environment and eventually one another. Unfortunately, slavery, bureaucracies, taxes, and the military draft are all rooted in the same revolution that made movies and video games possible.

WHAT ANTHROPOLOGICAL LINGUISTS DO

Learning a language you haven't previously studied in the place where it is spoken can be an exasperating experience, as you may know. But just think what it would be like to learn one in which the most basic vocabulary eluded you because it seemed even the native speakers did not agree on the right terms for the most commonly found objects!

For example, imagine that you point to an orange in a fruit market and the vendor asks, "pirani?" You nod to indicate this is what you want, and he puts the orange in a bag, then hands it to you.

Later when you proudly offer the fruit to an acquaintance, saying, "pirani?" he smiles indulgently, shakes his head, and, pointing to the orange corrects you by clearly enunciating "bajikan." Have you suddenly developed a hearing problem?

The next day you are offered an orange at the home of a professor. "Sampenaji?" asks the woman serving it to you. Is it a different variety of orange? No, it's identical to the others. And you are having the same problem with the words for other foods, parts of the body, pronouns and verbs of motion. You feel that you are the victim of a plot to keep you forever an outsider.

This is pretty much the situation anthropologist Clifford Geertz found himself in when he began learning one of the major languages spoken in Java. The problem was that the different words for the same object weren't merely synonyms that could be freely substituted for one another. What was going on here?

According to Geertz [see his book *The Religion of Java* (Glencoe, Ill.: The Free Press, 1960)], research finally revealed that what determined the correct choice of words was the social position of both speaker and listener. People of low status—peasants, for example—would use a particular vocabulary when speaking to their social equals, but were obligated to use another when addressing individuals of higher status, and still another for those of *very* high status.

People who occupied a middle position on the social ladder (such as merchants) also had three basic vocabularies: one for addressing their equals, one for those higher than themselves, and one for those lower. High-ranking people (such as government officials and judges) used different words, depending on whether they were conversing with equals, the low or the *very* low.

Were these different groups speaking different languages? Not at all. They understood one another perfectly well. And what's more, the vocabulary used by the low-ranking peasants to speak to one another was the one *everybody* used when talking with family or close friends.

Apparently Javanese speech is a powerful reflector of traditional Javanese culture, with its insistence on correct behavior toward people belonging to rigidly separate categories. Through their word choices the people continue to confirm differences of status among them.

Does English have this capacity? To a certain extent it does, though we aren't in the habit of thinking about it. One example is the vocabulary we use to address others. Consider, for instance, the different possible effects of calling a strange woman "ma'am," "sis," or "doll face." Probably if you think about it a while you could come up with other examples of how your style of speech shifts according to who's listening.

Trying to relate aspects of culture (such as beliefs about who owes whom respect) to the use of language, as it is spoken by all classes of people, is one of the jobs of anthropological linguists. For the more unfamiliar languages of the world, especially those with no tradition of writing, they also create dictionaries and *grammars*, the rules for combining the units of a language into meaningful words and sentences.

Finally, they try to unravel the historical relationships between languages. This entails charting the changes that have occurred in the sounds and meanings of words for clues about the changing relations between the people who uttered them. These anthropologists are the cultivators of our linguistic family trees.

WHAT CULTURAL ANTHROPOLOGISTS DO

Laura Bohannan, an English cultural anthropologist, was studying a village of Tiv tribespeople in Nigeria, West Africa, when the seasonal rains put an end to work in the fields. It was a time to just sit indoors and drink beer and gab.

One day as the rains came, an old man urged the anthropologist to tell a story from her land. Ms. Bohannan protested that she was not a good storyteller, but it was in vain. The audience that had already collected was up for a story, so she decided to tell the story of Hamlet as a kind of test of Shakespeare's supposed universality. Not only had her listerners never heard of Shakespeare; they knew almost nothing of the Western world.

At almost every point in the plot, the village elder interrupted to correct the storyteller's "mistakes." On the matter of Ophelia's drowning he was particularly certain she had gotten things wrong or had misunderstood. "Only witches can make people drown. Water," he assured her, "can't hurt anything. It's merely something one drinks and bathes in."

At this news, Ms. Bohannan stopped dead in her tracks, grabbed her notebook and began to write. The old man looked triumphant. He would succeed in educating this unusually ignorant young Westerner yet.

In many ways this was, until recently, a typical experience for the cultural anthropologist doing fieldwork in a far-off place.

You would arrive an unexpected stranger in a community where people's most basic beliefs about how the world operates were likely to be different from your own. You would be treated like a child by all the adults because apparently you knew about as much as a small child of that place, maybe even less.

Your long-term goal was to produce an *ethnography*, a written portrait of the society's community life as a whole. So for months you went about observing the daily activities of men, women, and children, systematically asking dozens of questions.

You took a census of the community and for each household constructed a *genealogy*, an in-depth history of the family members based on your conversations. Taken together, these genealogies would, you hoped, shed light on a number of subjects, including local patterns of marriage, divorce, and settlement (where people go to live after they marry).

Eventually you felt that you had become something of an expert on these people. Then somebody said something that made you realize you didn't even know enough to ask the really interesting questions!

Not all cultural anthropologists embark for distant shores. Some stay home and do the comparative part of the job. They sift through the ethnographies written by the travelers like miners panning for gold. Their aim is to discover cross-cultural patterns in marriage, child rearing, religious beliefs and practices, warfare—almost any subject imaginable. They often use their findings to argue for or against particular hypotheses about people worldwide. Cultural anthropologists who do this kind of comparative and interpretative research are called *ethnologists*.

CULTURE CHANGE

In recent years populations throughout the world have been brought closer together. Every day more tribespeople are being absorbed into towns and cities while the tentacles of modern technology and the mass media in particular extend to the most out-of-the-way places. New ideas and new ways of dealing with the land, other people, and the spirit world are being tried out everywhere. As a result it's no longer possible to say what the boundaries of a given culture are. No group today presents us with anything like a unique bundle of ideas and behavior.

The revolutionizing effects of modern technology on the world have revolutionized the thinking of many cultural anthropologists. They have come to realize that perhaps people were *never* as isolated or uninfluenced by other groups as was once believed.

By all recent indications, humans have been tramping about for millions of years. Surely even the early migrants helped to cross-fertilize ideas as well as genes. Maybe if it were possible even in the distant past to plot out the boundaries of the world's cultures, the correct model wouldn't be a rainbow after all. Maybe it would be a lava lamp, an ooze of slowly shape-shifting, interpenetrating elements.

Is the notion of culture then still the key to our self-knowledge as anthropologists once believed? In the following chapters we'll see how recent and revolutionizing finds within its subfields shape the answer to this question.

CHAPTER 3
PLANET OF THE APES REVISITED: ARE APES AND MONKEYS HUMAN?

*T*he apes that appeared on the screen in the movie *Planet of the Apes* could do just about everything. That included performing brain surgery on the human intruders who wandered into their territory.

By comparison, the achievements of real monkeys and apes—at least those observed in the wild—are much more modest. The apes that now receive special tutoring in human ways, on the other hand, show stunning progress. No one expects that they or even their offspring will have the grades to enter medical school, or that a population of apes more humanlike than we've ever known will evolve on its own. But we are getting a very different picture of what an ape is capable of learning with its relatively small brain. And as we'll see, this new picture can't but affect the way we look at fossils of our own ancestors.

Until quite recently, people cherished the idea that only human beings had culture. To believe otherwise was like opening to the world-at-large the doors of a posh and exclusive club. But the field studies of the past few decades make it difficult not to allow at least some monkeys and apes into the "culture club." For surely they have the beginnings of culture, what anthropologists call *protoculture*.

For a long time the making of tools and weapons was considered one of those things that only people did. Only people were thought smart enough to make them. And there was something more. When our ancestors first began to systematically make tools, they turned down a separate evolutionary path pointing to the modern world. In other words, tools made people as much as people make tools. Or so at least the theory went. You can just imagine the clamor that was caused by the discovery of tool-using, wild apes.

For an even longer time, language was thought to be an ability unique to humankind. It's only natural, therefore, that the real and growing prospect of our being able, like Dr. Dolittle, to "talk with the animals," has been met with a deluge of protests as well as delight.

But to start at the beginning of the primate "cultural revolution," we have to consider not the tool-making or language using apes, but a group of ground-dwelling wild monkeys in Japan. Among anthropologists they became famous for the unlikely reason that they wash their potatoes.

"CULTURE" AND THE JAPANESE MACAQUES OF KOSHIMA

Koshima is a small island in Kyushu, Japan. In 1950 it was the home of a number of different kinds of animals, including a troop of about twenty monkeys. They belonged to a group with the scientific but musical-sounding name *Macaca fuscata*. Since the scientific naming of animals is an issue of some importance and will be cropping up again and again in the following chapters, we should perhaps say something about it here.

Like most of you, all animals known to zoologists have been given at least two names. The second name (note that it is spelled with a small letter) tells you the *species* the animal belongs to. A species is really a breeding pool. In it are all those individuals whom—provided they are of the appropriate sex, the right age and in good health—a particular animal could successfully mate with.

Successful mating, in turn, is defined as the ability to produce fertile offspring. Horses and donkeys can mate, but their offspring, the mule, is always sterile and so can't continue either line. For this reason we consider horses and donkeys to be two separate species. The fact that they can mate shows that they have a close common ancestor, and perhaps at one point in the past they were a single species.

The first name of an animal refers to its *genus* (pronounced with a long *e*). A genus is nothing more than a bunch of different species which, in the opinion of scientists, appear to be similar in many ways. It is assumed that species of a single genus have a close common ancestry, and that perhaps at an earlier time they were one breeding population.

The dog (*Canis familiaris*) and the wolf (*Canis lupus*) have different species names because their habitats and life-styles generally make it impossible for them to mate. But they are so closely related that occasionally an Eskimo dog and a wolf do succeed in making music together (and, of course, making fertile pups, too). For this reason dogs and wolves have a common genus name: *Canis.*

To return to *Macaca fuscata.* In 1952, the Primate Research Group of Japan began to observe these animals on their little island. Not only did the humans observe and record the monkey-doings there. They began to provision the troop with food as well. As a result of these regular bonanzas, the troop's population tripled to fifty-nine in the next ten years. Furthermore, these macaques, as they are called, were becoming the gourmets of the simian world, developing a taste for foods no monkey in the wild ever got its hands on. And among the newly introduced foods were sweet potatoes.

There was nothing particularly surprising in the fact that the macaques came to relish sweet potatoes. Captive animals are known to acquire a taste for all kinds of food not native to them, including peanut-butter sandwiches. What was surprising was the behavior of one particular female named Imo', who in 1952 was only a year and a half old.

She would regularly take her potatoes to the edge of the water and there individually dip them in; then she would hold each potato in one hand and remove the sand from it by brushing it off with the other hand. Four years later, eleven

members of the troop were doing the same, and two years after that the number had risen to seventeen.

By 1958 an interesting change had taken place. In the earlier years the macaques would dip their food only at the edge of a small freshwater brook. Now they were using the seashore as well (even immersing themselves in the water, something most monkey species regularly avoid doing).

Here they would dip the potatoes into the saltwater after each bite. They seemed to prefer the saltwater, for they began to use the brook only if there were other animals hogging the beachfront. Researchers are convinced that the macaques are seasoning their food with salt, having discovered that it adds zest to the flavor!

By 1961, the troop had forty-nine members. Only two born before 1950 hadn't jumped on the potato-dipping wagon. Of the monkeys born after the great discovery of Imo', only four refrained from potato-dipping. Interestingly, they were all offspring of one of the two adult holdouts. Ultimately, it isn't the new behavior itself, but rather the manner in which it spread throughout the troop that gives us a provocative peek at how ideas might have caught on during our own early days, before language and the nuclear family were invented.

When Imo' began the potato-washing experiment, only the juveniles (those between one and two and a half) bothered to pay any attention to her. From then on, for the next four years, male troop members learned to wash their potatoes only if they were under the age of four. Females, on the other hand, picked it up regardless of their age; even some of the adults began imitating Imo' early on.

What explains this difference in learning? Are female macaques inherently brighter, more daring, more able to change their behavior than males? Not at all. As human females today know, the opportunity to learn something is as necessary to learning it as the biological capacity to. In order

Simian gourmet. A macaque of Koshima Island, Japan

to learn something from someone, you first have to have access to that someone.

When a male macaque becomes four years old, he begins to move from the central part of the troop to its periphery. That's where the big guys hang out together. But contrary to popular belief, males aren't alone in having a long history of grouping. Female primates, too, have a strong tendency to form groups of their own, groups which include their dependent youngsters. Sometimes three generations of females and their offspring travel close together. And those who spend lots of time together, invariably dine together. The youngsters were the closest to young Imo', and those closest to them were their moms.

What happened at Koshima, at least in the beginning, was this: the invention of potato-washing was transmitted from the young to the old through offspring-to-mother ties. After 1959, when potato-dipping had ceased to be a fad, but had become an established practice with proven benefits to taste as well, the method of transmission was reversed. For youngsters that began to learn it from their mothers during their earliest days, potato-dipping became a normal feeding pattern.

Is this really "culture"? Yes and no. The washing and seasoning of potatoes by Koshima's macaques are behaviors that are clearly learned. They are also shared by troop members but not outsiders. By definition this makes the behavior "cultural."

Is it fair to say Koshima macaques *have* a culture, are therefore human? Of course not. Culture isn't a discrete package that we acquired all at once like a birthday present. We talk about it as if it were, but clearly it is something else: a process by which *most* of what we know came to be learned and not transmitted through the genes. To be truly cultural, monkeys will have to soup up something more than salted raw potatoes.

CHIMPANZEES AND TOOLS

At the same time that the Primate Research Group in Japan was concluding its ten-year survey of the gourmet macaques, the young Jane Goodall was setting out with her mother to have the first prolonged scientific look at chimpanzees in the wild. She chose to study a group of *Pan troglodytes*, the long-haired variety that dwells in a rugged, mountainous, sparsely populated region of Africa (hence its species name meaning "hermit"). The habitat of the particular troop was the Gombe Stream Reserve, a chimpanzee sanctuary bordering the shores of Lake Tanganyika in Tanzania.

In a relatively short time, the newcomer was able to differentiate the members of "her" troop. One day through her binoculars she saw something no Westerner had ever before seen. A chimp—the one she called David Greybeard—was squatting beside a large termite mound. Says Dr. Goodall:

> . . . as I watched I saw him carefully pass a long green stem down into a hole in the mound. After a moment he withdrew it and picked something from the end of his mouth.

That "something" proved to be . . . termites! When the human observer was sure that animal had left, she went to examine the mound.

> I picked up one of his discarded tools and carefully pushed it into a hole myself. Immediately I felt the pull of several termites as they seized the grass, and when I pulled it out there were a number of worker termites and a few soldiers with big red heads clinging on. . . . There they remained, sticking out at right angles to the stem with their legs waving in the air.

Sucking homemade termite lollipops wasn't the habit of just a single, inventive chimp, at least by the time of the first observation. Dr. Goodall also describes how a pair of troop mates "fished" together for two hours:

> . . . they scratched open the sealed-over passage entrances with a thumb or forefinger. I watched how

they bit the end off their tools when they became bent, or used the other end, or discarded them in favor of new ones. Goliath once moved at least 15 yards from the heap to select a firm-looking piece of vine, and both males often picked three or four stems while they were collecting tools, and put the spare ones beside them on the ground until they wanted them.

Sometimes the animals couldn't find suitable grass stems. When that happened they did something that staggered anthropologists when it was first reported. The chimps searched out a slender leafy twig and proceeded to systematically remove all the leaves. When this was done, they had a nice clean pole with which to go termite fishing!

The chimps were not only using tools; they were *making* them. They were modifying natural objects for a purpose other than the one nature intended, a purpose that took root inside their own imaginations. This was big news. Toolmaking was supposed to be uniquely human. *Man, the Toolmaker* was a famous book on the Stone Age. *Man and Chimp, The Toolmakers* did not have quite the same ring. Either the definition of "human" would have to be altered, or else, as the late paleontologist Louis Leakey pointed out, we'd have to accept chimps into the human family.

Jane Goodall discovered that the Gombe chimps also used stones to hammer open nuts, and sticks as levers to enlarge the openings of underground bees' nests. (Later they used these to open the treasure chests of bananas that she herself began to leave for them.) She also found them using something else as a tool. One day the male called Evered was peering into what seemed to be the hollow of a tree. Dr. Goodall observed:

He picked a handful of leaves, chewed them for a moment, took them out of his mouth and pushed

Dr. Jane Goodall and a precocious member of a Gombe Stream chimpanzee troop

them down into the hollow. Quickly Evered sucked the liquid from his home made sponge and pushed it into the hollow once more.

The Gombe chimps also use their leaf-made sponges for a more conventional purpose: for wiping. With them they clean their hands of sticky substances or dab at bleeding wounds. And finally, chimps suffering from diarrhea use their leafy sponges as toilet paper: a helpful hint to bear in mind if you're ever lost in a rain forest and forced to survive on ba-nanas.*

TALKING APES

The idea of teaching an ape to speak English was put into motion in the 1940s by an American couple, Catherine and Keith Hayes. From the films that were made of this project, it is clear that their pupil, a chimpanzee named Viki, was making a heroic effort to comply with the humans' bizarre (from her point of view) demands.

For example, the Hayeses claimed that the word "cup" was part of Viki's vocabulary. But what one hears are only the first and last consonants of the word pronounced rather separately. And as one anthropologist has pointed out, what one sees on-screen is a chimp whose distorted face and head position suggest those of an individual about to be tortured rather than one about to engage in spontaneous conversation. It became evident to everyone who followed the Hayes' experiment that however bright and motivated, chimps lack the vocal apparatus (at the very least) to make the sounds of human language.

Field studies of the early 1960s revealed that primates in the wild convey a good deal of information to one another, but much of this communication isn't vocal at all. The animals rely instead on the kinds of intimacy we humans fall back on when words fail us. That is to say, they hug and kiss a lot, pat one another, finger one another's fur. We come from a family that goes in for "hands-on" therapy in a big way.

*Tool use among wild chimpanzees is described in Jane Goodall's book *In the Shadow of Man* (New York: Dell, 1971).

Realizing that this might have important implications for chimpanzee education, another American couple, Beatrice and R. Allen Gardner, began in 1966 to teach a young female chimp American Sign Language. Washoe, as she was called, made history. In the course of three years of instruction, she mastered at least eighty-five signs. That she did indeed understand these signs was verified through a method called "double blind" testing. This is the way it works:

One person presents the object (or picture of an object) which the animal is to be tested on. Then he or she leaves the room. The animal is then allowed to enter through a separate door. Another assistant enters, stands behind the partitioned object or image so that he or she can't see it, and asks the chimp: "what is this?" The animal's signed response is recorded.

The procedure is repeated for each tested item. (In the case of flashed images on the screen, there is no need for the first person to keep entering and leaving.) At no time does the animal see the teacher who presents the image or object, and at no time does the assistant doing the recording see the object or image the animal is responding to. This eliminates the possibility of the teacher unconsciously cueing the chimp to help the pupil get an *A*.

Inspired by Washoe and other chimps who have since learned sign language and some computer keyboard skills, Francine Patterson tackled the rather more formidable task of teaching them to a gorilla. In 1972, she became both "mother" and teacher to a year-old, zoo-born female gorilla named Koko.* It was the beginning of a relationship that is as special in its own way, as King Kong's was to Fay Wray.

After three years, Koko could correctly use 127 different signs. Many of them were words which she also understood in English, for like Washoe, she was regularly exposed to the sounds of a spoken English word at the same time that the sign for it was molded in her hand.

Impressive as the size of her vocabulary may seem, it doesn't come close to expressing the gorilla's real knowl-

*The descriptions that follow of Koko's abilities are drawn from *The Education of Koko*, by Francine Patterson and Eugene Linden (New York: Holt, Rinehart & Winston, 1981).

edge. As her teacher explains, like most bright students, Koko finds the repetition of word drills and tests exasperating. Asked what she thought was boring, after a long session on the words for body parts, she signed: *Think eye ear eye nose boring.* When she doesn't want to be drilled or tested anymore, she may turn off the videotape machine or tape recorder and walk away. She is the underachiever of the gorilla world.

Ms. Patterson believes that what Koko's critics dismiss as her "mistakes" are really a window into the gorilla's mind. She says that Koko enjoys playing with the language and has been known to make jokes. Here is an example:

> Koko was making a nest out of white towels and as she arranged the towels, Barbara noticed that Koko was signing *"red."* Barbara said, "You know better, Koko. What color is it?" Koko insisted that it was red, signing *"red"* three times, each sign larger than the preceding. Then, with a grin, she picked up a minute speck of red lint that had been clinging to the towel and held it up to Barbara's face, signing *"red."*

Koko also expresses her fears accurately. Asked at one point what makes her afraid, she signed, *alligator.* She has never seen a live alligator, but she is genuinely terrified of Patterson's pet iguana. Pictures of alligators and toy plastic or rubber alligators send her into a panic.

Jane Goodall is convinced that chimpanzees in the wild understand something about death, that they experience profound grief when it takes those close to them. Perhaps the most remarkable example of how language can crystallize ideas—in this case ideas about death—comes from this signed conversation between Koko and one of her instructors. The pupil was asked to pick out the gorilla from a set of pictures showing skeletons of four different animals. Koko

Nim Chimpsky conversing in American Sign Language with his teacher, Joyce Butler

correctly identified it. Then she was asked if the gorilla was alive or dead. Koko signed: *Dead, good-bye.* Next she was asked how gorillas feel when they die: happy, sad, or afraid. Koko replied: *Sleep.* Instructor: Where do gorillas go when they die? Koko: *Comfortable hole bye.* Maureen: When do gorillas die? Koko: *Trouble old.*

We know for a fact that wild gorillas do not bury their dead, and even if they did Koko wouldn't know about it, having lived her entire life in captivity. How then did she come to associate skeletons with holes in the ground? The answer according to her teacher is that Koko is an avid fan of *National Geographic.*

CHAPTER 4
WHO IS LUCY?

Ascene in the movie *2001: A Space Odyssey* shows a crowd of apish-looking, humanlike creatures watching in awe as one of them brandishes a club against another. They are in awe because they are the first ever to witness the power of weaponry. The event is a turning point for the evolution of humanity. The film lets us know this by showing the repeated downward thrust of the creature's arm as he smashes his target to smithereens in slow motion and to the sound of grandiose music.

Unlike the humanlike teddy bear Ewoks of *The Empire Strikes Back*, the characters in *2001* were inspired by what anthropology was at the time saying about our *hominid* ancestors.

Hominid is a term which anthropologists use to categorize not only ourselves, but also those extinct beings who, on the bases of their bones and teeth, appear to have been more like us than like apes. As you can see, it's a rather judgmental term. How humanlike did the creatures have to be? Human in what ways? And how can we know anything about their ideas and ways of behaving from bare bones?

For a long time there were no answers to these questions, or rather there were too many, which comes to the same thing. That was because for decades the sparse array of fossils that were the learning blocks for the early anthropologists served only to create dissension among them. With the discovery of more fossils filling in the gaps of the picture, old debates could finally be settled. Among other things, today's anthropologists more or less agree on what a hominid is.

But don't get the idea that new finds always resolve questions. Just as often they fuel new disputes about their interpretation. Debate is to anthropology what oxygen is to living organisms.

EARLY HOMINID FOSSILS

It was Thomas Huxley back in the nineteenth century who first said that Africa would be a good place to look for fossils of extinct kinds of apes. But no one took him up on the suggestion for the excellent reason that African apes live in dense forests, where excavating is difficult. Besides, fossils of such great antiquity would be more likely to be preserved in caves. No one thought to look in South Africa, where the forests had disappeared long ago and presumably with them all traces of the apes that lived in them. By the turn of the century the "missing link" between apes and humans was being sought in Asia. But it was in South Africa, where no one had been looking, that some of the earliest hominids once dwelt, and it was there that their existence was first discovered.

Like many other wonderful discoveries, it was the result of an inquisitive and informed mind coming together—largely through chance—with a piece of a thing that was not supposed to exist. But as usual, that was just the beginning. What was then required was the painstaking labor to find the other pieces and to make sense of the whole. Only then would the "discovery" be publicly worthy of the term. Such was the sequence of events in store for Raymond Dart, professor of anatomy in Johannesburg, South Africa in 1924.

AUSTRALOPITHECUS,
THE "SOUTHERN APE"

It all began that year with the visit of a college student to a friend's house. Noticing a new addition to the mantelpiece, she asked if it were the skull of a baboon. The friend replied that there were no monkey or ape fossils in South Africa. He didn't know what it was, but it came from a limestone cave that he owned in a place nearby called Taung.

The student reported the story to one of her professors. Being interested in fossils himself, he asked her to tell the friend he'd be pleased to have a peek at any that turned up at Taung in the future.

It was in this way that two crates full of bone fragments and debris turned up one day at the home of Raymond Dart. Most of the contents proved uninteresting, but finally there was something that only a trained eye such as his could have recognized as pay dirt. It was an *endocranial cast*—limestone that had over time solidified inside a skull—so that even though the skull itself was missing, he had before him something which in size and shape represented the braincase of its long-deceased owner.

Dart's first thought was that it was a baboon. (These ground-dwelling monkeys were known to have inhabited South Africa long ago.) Then he realized it was a bit too big, and besides, the shape wasn't quite right. In the second box he found a piece that fitted the cast. This enabled him to look at the animal's face, but it was so covered by a thick mixture of limestone, sand, and gravel (known as "breccia") that he could not make out its features no matter how hard he stared.

Not really knowing how to remove this masking substance, knowing only that he needed to learn the identity of the animal sitting before him, Dart proceeded, with some trepidation and much care, to hammer away at the breccia. At first he worked with a small chisel, then with one of his wife's knitting needles. The process took months, but finally there was a clean face looking back at him.

It was not that of a baboon, nor of any known monkey or ape. He knew that from the telltale teeth, especially the canines (the large, single-cusped teeth that are so prominent in dogs). These tend to be long in nonhuman primates, and the ones Dart was looking at were impossibly small. They were more like those of a six-year-old human child than anything else.

Something else perplexed Dart. The *foramen magnum*—that is, the hole in the skull through which the spinal column passes to ascend into the brain—was at the bottom, not at the back where it occurs in a four-legged animal like a dog. This creature carried its head above its spine the way we do. That meant it was *bipedal*; it walked erect.

Though this may seem like a lot to conclude from a mere hole, it was all Dart had to go on. There were no leg bones, no pelvic bones. The only problem was there were also no apes that regularly went about on two feet. And it would indeed be strange if apes had done so in the past but had somehow managed to lose the skill.

The creature, Dart reasoned, had to have been something between an ape and a human. He christened it *Australopithecus africanus*, meaning "Southern ape from Africa." (The name was a strange choice, for it didn't exactly broadcast the humanlike qualities Dart was so taken with.) On the basis of other animal fossils found in the same cave, he reported the extraordinary find to be an estimated one million years old.

Almost no one in the scientific community of the time was very impressed. Its members did not agree with Dart's assessments of the fossil. In fact, there wasn't much they did agree on. This was only normal. They were also trying to make sense of later, but equally perplexing, bones from around the world. Scientific methods of dating fossils had not yet been discovered, and the bones themselves were often fragmentary and badly damaged.

To complicate things further, the sparse sample represented individuals who lived on different continents during an enormous time span. Their relationship to one another was unknown. The task of discovering it was equal to that of trying to chart the precise movements of a vanished herd of mad giraffes from their fast-fading footprints in sand.

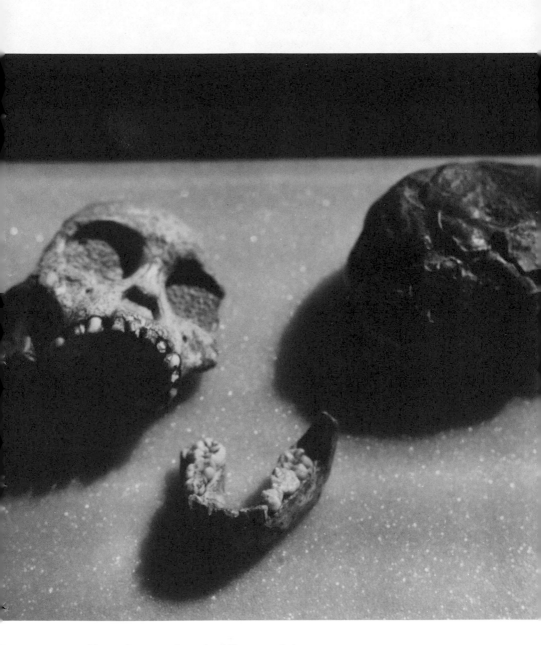

*Face, jaw, and cast of the cranial
cavity of the Taung baby*

Over the next four years Dart tried to separate the jaws of the "Taung Baby" (as his fossil came to be popularly known) so as to get a better look at the chewing surfaces of its teeth. When at last he was able to, he knew his "baby" was a surefire hominid. Again he wrote, this time describing the humanlike teeth. Still, almost no one took the fossil seriously.

One reason was that the skull belonged to a youngster, and the bone structures of human and ape youngsters were known to be more alike than those of adults. But there was another reason. A brainy ancestor with apelike teeth was considered a far more socially acceptable addition to the human family tree. And a fossil with just this combination of features had turned up years before in England.

PILTDOWN MAN

Referred to as *Piltdown Man* (because it had been found in a place called Piltdown), this fossil consisted of a human-proportioned brain with an apish jaw, but one that contained manlike teeth. In other words, in its main features it was the exact opposite of *Australopithecus*. The situation was baffling even to the experts. Debate over the meaning of the two fossils raged on.

Eventually in the 1950s it was discovered that Piltdown Man wasn't an authentic fossil at all, but rather the instrument of an elaborate hoax. Whoever had committed the forgery had skillfully attached a 500-year-old human skull to the jaw of an orangutan, flattened the ape's teeth with a file to make them look human, dyed the fossil to make it appear old, and then buried it in a fossil-rich site along with the bone of a mastodon (an extinct elephantlike mammal) now known to have come from Tunisia!

The Taung Baby's status as a hominid was strengthened when other Australopithecus bones, including those of adults, began to turn up in Africa. These creatures were small! Alive they weighed between 50 pounds (23 kilograms) and 90 pounds (41 kilograms) and measured about 4 feet (1.2 meters).

OTHER FINDS

During the 1950s, in a cave not far from where hominid fossils were found, Raymond Dart discovered the remains of ancient baboons. A disproportionate number of them had skulls that had been struck on the left side. This seemed most peculiar to Dart and not likely to be due to coincidence. He proposed that the skulls had been smashed by right-handed australopithecines (hominids of the genus *Australopithecus*) wielding bone weapons. He had begun to picture these hominids as ferocious hunters, a view which the mass media and the public eagerly adopted.

But many scientists, especially those who'd had experience with baboons in the wild, were unconvinced. They knew how difficult these animals are to approach. Alert, intelligent and long of tooth, they almost always hang about in groups, and they have a deeply ingrained habit of protecting one another. The image of them quietly allowing shrimpy australopithecines to sneak up and bop them over the heads was, to some, the most unlikely scenario ever conjured by an anthropologist. An adult baboon would have to be anesthetized to permit such a direct approach. Australopithecines may have been smart, but they weren't that smart!

Others, even today, are convinced that the baboon skulls in question *were* cracked due to a frontal assault rather than due to falling rocks. Perhaps, they say, the animals were asleep when the maneuver took place. They also point out that there is evidence that the brains were picked and eaten. This is not unheard of among humans, but in this case the picking is attributed to the australopithecines who presumably also did the bopping.

Just how smart could these hominids have been? In actual size their brains were comparable to those of chimps and gorillas. Those that can be measured range from 428 cubic centimeters to 530 cubic centimeters. In comparison, the *cranial size* (that is, the volume of the skull) of human adults ranges from 1,000 to 2,500 cubic centimeters. But absolute size may not be a fair indication of australopithecine intelligence. They were smaller than apes, and apparently it is the proportion of an animal's brain size to body weight that is important.

We, of course, don't really know for sure what the australopithecines or their immediate ancestors were like. But recently, some physical anthropologists have come to believe that the best living model we have for the common ancestor of hominids, chimps, and gorillas is *Pan paniscus*, popularly known as the pygmy chimpanzee.

On the average, pygmy chimpanzees weigh less than common chimps. They are comparable in overall body size and skull features to Australopithecus, although the latter had a larger brain capacity. Compared with other chimps, the pygmies display fewer physical differences between the sexes, and in captivity they spend more time walking upright.

As more hominid fossils were discovered, anthropologists argued about what the differences among them signified and how the different specimens should be classified. Two distinct types kept cropping up. One had smaller back teeth and a more slender bone structure. *Australopithecus africanus* was the name settled on for this group.

The second was called *Australopithecus robustus.* As its name suggests, these characters were a good deal burlier, at least by the standards of their day. Also, not only were their back teeth larger and more specialized, they had thicker, more massive jaws and muscle attachments. These suggest that they did some awfully powerful chewing, probably of roots and stalks.

Leaving aside the problem of the other fossils that didn't fit neatly into either group (being intermediary in their bone structure), these two in and of themselves presented a puzzle. From their relative dating, it appeared that the apish-looking robustus was more recent in time than the more human-looking *africanus*! What was going on here? No one could say for sure. Then in the 1960s and 1970s the answers came, gradually but with the impact of lightning bolts, and this time not from South Africa, but from East Africa.

AUSTRALOPITHECUS *IN EAST AFRICA*

Hot and desolate Olduvai Gorge in Tanzania, East Africa, is a 300-foot (91-meter) layer cake of rock. Its different strata were chiseled by the flow of ancient rivers that are no more. At one time, however, there was no layer cake, only a lake. Its life-sustaining waters attracted all kinds of animals who made its shore their home, and in the 1930s the place attracted two doughty fossil hunters: Kenyan-born Louis Leakey and his wife, Mary.

It wasn't only the fossils that brought them back year after year, but some of the chipped stones. Looking at them you couldn't have told them apart from the million others lying about and so you would not have been impressed. But to knowing eyes, these were special stones. It wasn't the weather that had caused their chipping, but a hand and mind not fundamentally different from our own. They were the crudest-looking stone tools still worthy of the name that have ever been found. We assume they were used for chopping things.

The Leakeys wanted to prove that the early hominids had made these tools. And so they became obsessed with finding their fossils in the same strata in which they had found the stones.

It happened in the summer of 1959. It was Mary who found the skull, though the news caused Louis to fly from his sickbed and scamper feverishly across the gorge to see it. It was Mary, too, who spent the next several months reconstructing the whole from its many fragments.

The skull made the name of Leakey famous overnight, for its association with stone tools overturned completely certain lines of thinking about human origins.

By now the scientific community accepted australopithecines as hominids, but hominids that represented a weird, dead-end shoot on the family tree. Not many people wanted beings with such puny brains as grandparents. The news that they actually made tools hit like a bomb.

At that time it was thought that only humans used tools. (This was before Jane Goodall's study of wild chimps.) Erect walking, the working of stone, and human intelligence were all thought to have developed together. But here was someone who walked on two feet, made tools, in short was human, without nearly enough brainpower to *be* human. If one admitted that apes had human potential in their brains, where did that leave us?

*Paleontologist Louis Leakey at
Olduvai Gorge, Tanzania*

In the fossil record, sandwiched in time between *Australopithecus* and ourselves, is another extinct hominid called *Homo erectus*. In Latin its genus name means "Man," what we mean by "human." Until recently, the earliest *Homo erectus* finds went back only half a million years. So when australopithecines came to be found in the same locations as *Homo erectus* fossils, some anthropologists concluded that *Australopithecus* was their direct ancestor.

But not the Leakeys. They hypothesized the existence of a more humanlike antecedent of *Homo erectus*, a human older than any *erectus* find.

In 1964 it seemed that their prophecy had come true. From Olduvai came news of a bonanza Leakey find: the remains of four hominids that seemed to fit the bill. It appeared as if these hominids had lived alongside the australopithecines. Anthropologists began to think that they, not the australopithecines, had made the stone tools. There was a collective sigh of relief. But not for long. The braincases of these fossils weren't a whole lot larger than those of the australopithecines; they measured an average of only 642 cubic centimeters. "Too small to be Homo!" shouted some. But Louis Leakey disagreed and called them *Homo habilis*, meaning 'Handy Man'. One thing about these hominids stunned everybody: their age.

CHEMICAL DATING

Paleoanthropology at this time was given a big boost by a real revolution in the chemical dating of remains. Called the *potassium argon method*, it became, for those who discovered hominid fossils in layers of volcanic ash, by turn a godsend and a bedevilment. This is how it works:

When a sample of volcanic ash in which a fossil has been found is put into a vacuum-tight machine and heated up with electricity, it melts and releases all of the argon gas that has been trapped in it since the ash was first laid down.

The argon is caused by the decay of radioactive potassium. This substance is found in tiny quantities in the air and even our bodies. Radioactive potassium has a known *half-life*—the amount of time it takes to decay into another element. That time is 1.3 billion years. In other words, of the remaining radioactive potassium in the air today, half of it will be used up in 1.3 billion years. It will have turned into argon.

There isn't enough potassium in hominid fossils to measure their age directly, but it is possible to know from the amount of argon released from uncontaminated volcanic ash the approximate age of that ash, and indirectly the age of something deposited in it when it was first laid down.

The date the computer registered for the *Homo habilis* finds was 1.75 million years, nearly twice the supposed age of the earliest australopithecines! But here was a new dilemma. How could *Homo* be older than its ancestor?

RECENT DISCOVERIES

The late 1960s and early 1970s saw the excavation of the Omo River beds in Ethiopia. There an international team under the direction of F. Clark Howell found more than 200 hominid fossils.

Among them, at two million years, were examples of *Australopithecus africanus*; slightly later than that *Homo habilis* first appeared. At 1.5 million years there was *Australopithecus robustus*, and half a million years later the first entrance of *Homo erectus*. It was beginning to look as though the record made some sense after all when the staggering news broke of another Leakey find, this time by their son, Richard.

The skull he found near Lake Turkana in Kenya and which was simply called "1470" (its catalogue number) was very human-looking. It measured 775 cubic centimeters. Richard Leakey announced that it was a *Homo* find without suggesting a second name. Again it was the fossil's age, determined by potassium argon testing, that made people gasp. The computer registered 2.9 million years! How could something so humanlike have preceded the australopithecines? Anthropologists were again thrown into a state of bafflement.

Then in the mid 1970s came the most dramatic finds to date. Among them is Lucy, the best-preserved hominid fossil

The Leakeys in 1959 working to piece together
the famous hominid skull found by Mary at
Olduvai Gorge. The skull had to be recon-
structed from hundreds of fragments.

we have, being nearly half of a complete adult skeleton. She was found by Donald Johanson and members of his research team at a site called Hadar in the Afar region of Ethiopia.

Lucy is very, very small, measuring about three and a half feet (a little over a meter) tall. When alive, she probably weighed about 60 pounds (27 kilograms). Despite her tiny brain, she walked as well as you do. And that was 3.5 million years ago!

Nearby other hominids were found, though none as small or as thoroughly intact as Lucy. As a group, Donald Johanson describes them in this way:

(They had) smallish, essentially human bodies with heads that were more ape-shaped than human-shaped. Their jaws were large and forward thrusting. . . . The upper parts of their faces were small and chimplike. . . . Male or female, they probably were hairier than modern humans. How much hairier cannot be determined. The color of their skins is also unknown but was probably dark, since the skin of gorillas, chimpanzees and all tropical humans is dark.

Lucy and her neighbors are sufficiently different from all other fossil hominids to warrant a brand-new name: *Australopithecus afarensis.* Donald Johanson and many other physical anthropologists believe they were the ancestors of *Australopithecus africanus.**

And what of the wrench thrown into the family tree by Skull 1470?

It now appears that the date originally given of 2.9 million years was in error. In succeeding potassium argon tests the computer gave a figure closer to two million. The machinery is not faulty, only extremely sensitive. It requires samples of ash uncontaminated by materials that inflate the age of the fossil, and it is very difficult to provide these.

*You can read more about Lucy and "friends" in *Lucy: The Beginnings of Humankind,* by Donald Johanson and Maitland Edey (New York: Warner Books, 1981).

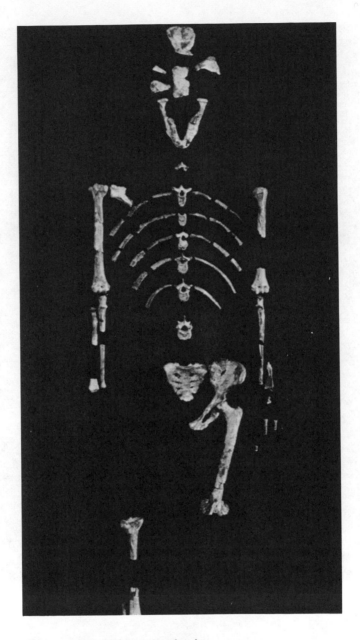

The remains of Lucy, who is about 3.5 million years old

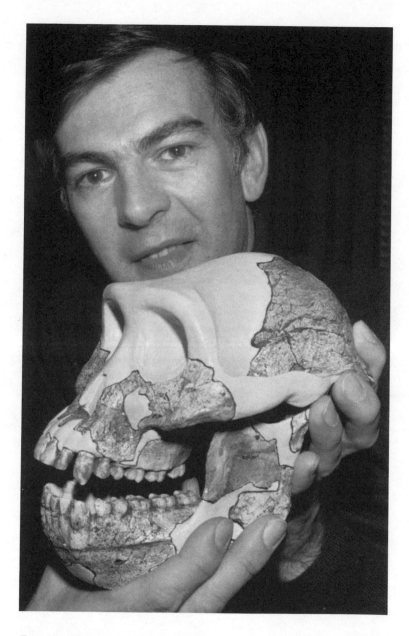

*Donald Johanson displaying
a plaster cast of Lucy's skull*

These 3.6-million-year-old footprints from Laetoli, Tanzania,
have been filled in with black
sand so that they can be better
seen in photographs. Whoever
made them had feet just like ours.

What now seems clear is that erect walking developed much earlier than anyone ever suspected and that it had nothing to do with the making of tools or the enlargement of the brain. Lucy's bones loudly proclaim this. But we also have another and rarer testament.

In 1976 the East African site called Laetoli, excavated by a team under the direction of Mary Leakey, produced a series of more than fifty parallel footprints covering a distance of 75 feet (23 meters). They were made by two hominids, one having slightly larger feet than the other. Perhaps it's the oldest record of a stroll taken by a pair of lovers, a gift of time coupled with the fact that they chose to walk on new-fallen ash that would suddenly solidify. Their relationship, the reason for their walk, and their way of perceiving the world will forever remain mysteries. But the message the footprints scream at us is: "Human feet!"

CHAPTER 5
HUMAN
AT LAST

*I*magine that for some reason all the places in the world where there are silkworms have been closed to trade and as a result no silk is available. Although you know almost nothing about silkworms, you take a sudden interest in them and decide they must exist in a place where no one has ever bothered to look for them. On the basis of climate you have a hunch they can be found in, say, Java. But you haven't the money to get there. So you join the Marines, hoping in this way to get near the place and investigate. As it turns out, after a series of mishaps that actually lead you closer to your goal, you are monumentally successful and return home a celebrity.

If this were a movie, we'd accept it as only an adventure fantasy, but these are close to the actual circumstances surrounding the first discovery of *Homo erectus*, the next hominid in our line.

THE "ERECT-WALKING APE-MAN"

In 1890, the anatomist Eugene Dubois decided to quit his teaching job in Holland and search for what at that time was

Timeline showing development of humankind, from *Australopithecus afarensis* to *Homo sapiens*

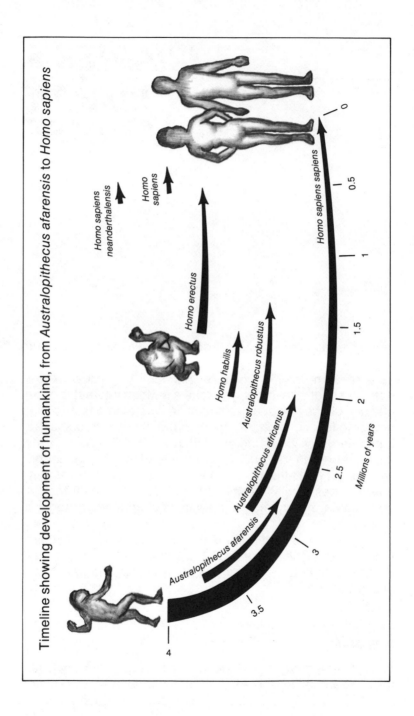

only a phrase—"the missing link." He had heard that on the island of Sumatra in Indonesia there was a species of man-like ape, the orangutan. He also heard that there were caves.

To Dubois it made sense to search for the bones in Asia rather than in Europe, where the Ice Age would have vanquished all trace of them. The only problem was getting to Sumatra, which was halfway around the world. So he joined the Dutch army as a military doctor and had himself posted to Indonesia (then controlled by the Dutch), more specifically to Sumatra.

There he soon contracted malaria and was transferred to Java, another island not far away, to recover. While in Java, Dubois began to dig near the Solo River. The Dutch Government became interested in what he was doing and lent him the use of a convict work force. Unfortunately for Dubois and anthropology, the prisoners discovered a more profitable use of the fossils they were digging up. They could sell them to Chinese traders who then ground them into powder and sold them as expensive medicines and aphrodisiacs: substances believed to increase the sexual appetites of those who consumed them. This has led anthropologists to wonder how many important fossils disappeared down the throats of nineteenth century Chinese thrill-seekers.

After a year of systematic digging, Dubois unearthed a single tooth, and somewhat later part of a skull too heavy to be that of a modern human. The next year, only yards away, a femur (upper leg bone) was found which showed that its owner walked erect. Dubois was convinced they all belonged to the same individual and that he had found the "missing link." He called it *Pithecanthropus erectus*, or "Erect-walking Ape-Man."

He returned to Europe in triumph, but the glory was short-lived. At first the center of a lively controversy, "Java Man," as the fossil came to be called, was soon dismissed by the scientific community as nothing more than a modern human, albeit a primitive looking one. In disgust, Dubois buried the fossil under the floorboards of his dining room, and, according to anthropologist Donald Johanson, "for thirty years refused to show it to scientists or to speak to them about it."

Later finds in Java, made mostly between 1936 and 1941, proved Dubois correct in his belief in the great antiquity of the bones. They showed that *Pithecanthropus erectus*, whose name was eventually changed to *Homo erectus*, persisted in Java, largely unchanged for half a million years. Furthermore, this hominid is the very first that is known to have journeyed beyond the borders of Africa, the center of human evolution, where the oldest of them are found. Rather quickly, they made their way to China, to Java (then connected to the Asian mainland), and probably even to Europe.

Just how old is *Homo erectus*? Recently in East Turkana, Kenya, Richard Leakey discovered the most complete *Homo erectus* skull we have. It has been dated at 1.5 million years, making it a million years older than the Java fossils and half a million older than those of the Ethiopian Omo beds!

The discovery of such an old *erectus* requires us to push back even further the time at which we draw the human/nonhuman distinction. The net effect of these revisions is to dramatically alter our thinking about human origins. We have spent more time on earth as humans than we used to imagine. Evolutionarily, we aren't the late bloomers we once thought we were.

And what did *Homo erectus* look like? On the average they were 6 inches (15 centimeters) taller than the australopithecines. They also had pronounced *brow ridges*; that is, they had a bar of bone extending over and across their eye sockets. And the region where their neck muscles attached to the skull was greatly expanded; they had powerful neck muscles. In fact, almost all of their bones were unusually thick. They must have been quite a muscular lot.

Most important of all, *Homo erectus* was big-brained. The skulls range in size from 700 to 1200 cubic centimeters. This is still small when compared with those of modern people, but the two ranges overlap. *Homo erectus* is also credited with a revolution in the manufacturing of tools.

THE ACHEULIAN INDUSTRY

At Olduvai Gorge in the levels occupied about 1.5 million years ago, a change can be seen in the kind of stone tools that appear. The simple, crudely flaked, unimpressive choppers give way to more complex and better-made tools, tools that even an ordinary person can recognize as such. Taken together they form what is called the *Acheulian industry.*

Among the new implements are those made from flakes which were in turn struck off from prepared cores of stone. Most abundant are examples of the pear-shaped, all-purpose tool referred to as a hand-axe or "biface" (so called because the two edges that form the point are the ones that have been worked). This has been described as a Stone Age scout's knife. We are fairly sure that it was used for cutting, digging, chopping, woodworking and drilling. As time went on its manufacture became more refined. Other new tools appear as well, some of which were regularly resharpened after use.

The big question raised by the presence of these tools—and/or weapons—is: what else, if anything, was *Homo erectus* doing with them? Here there is a major split in the thinking of today's anthropologists. It is a split that is so important to the way in which we all view our origins *and* our present-day behavior that the next chapter is devoted to exploring the two sides.

Essentially the division is between those who accept the traditional view that hunting is a deeply rooted part of our evolutionary history, going back to *Homo erectus* times (if not longer), and those who see it as a relatively recent way of life that came about only in the past 25,000 to 50,000 years.

Those who argue that early hominid populations earned their living largely through hunting are associated with what one anthropologist has dubbed the "Tarzan school of thinking." They believe that men have been the major providers for women and children for virtually all of our human history.

Some go further and say that we acquired many of our distinctive human traits because *Homo erectus* males became serious hunters. That is to say, we lost most of our bodily hair, became much more intelligent and developed different sex roles as direct consequences of the hunting way of life.

The opposing school of thought is championed by those

who believe that on the contrary, females were responsible for much of their groups' provisioning and that their efforts, as much as those of their male companions, contributed to the survival and evolution of the earliest human populations.

The question of who regularly did what (for example, did *Homo erectus* men hunt alone while women stayed behind, or did the two sexes join forces?) cannot easily be gathered from the fossil record. All we have are the ancient bones. But these bones do tell us some interesting things.

HOMO ERECTUS
IN CHINA

Half a million years ago, a limestone cave near Peking called Chou Kou Tien was home to at least fourteen individuals identified from their fossil remains as *Homo erectus*.

On the floor of the cave the bones of over ninety species of animals were also found. Most prominent were the bones of red deer, but there were also signs of pigs, sheep, bison, rhinoceros, buffalo, and a kind of giant beaver.

Stone tools, mostly flakes and choppers, also were present. A widespread assumption is that *Homo erectus* males went out and killed these large beasts and brought them home for dinner. Yet none of the artifacts found in the cave is clearly associated with hunting—only with the butchering and preparing of food. Vast concentrations of hackberry seeds suggest that these were probably a staple.

The four thick layers of ash found at Chou Kou Tien have led most experts to believe that its inhabitants knew how to use fire. Although some of the bones in the cave were charred, suggesting the cave dwellers preferred their rhinos cooked, the ash layers aren't regular enough to prove that *Homo erectus* could make a fire at will.

The animal bones weren't the only ones that were charred; a number of the human ones were, too. Because of this, some anthropologists suspect that the inhabitants were practicing cannibalism. The evidence, which was never entirely clear, is in any case no longer available. During the first days of World War II, the bones from Chou Kou Tien

Excavation at the Chou Kou Tien site in China

vanished in yet another of anthropology's unsolved mysteries.

The reopening of China to Western scientists is an event that couldn't be more welcome to American paleoanthropologists. They anticipate that excavations soon to be under way in that country will help give us an even better picture than we now have of the infancy of our genus.

THE NEANDERTHALERS

Call someone a "Neanderthaler" and most likely that person will take offense. The term refers to a human population that lived between 35,000 and 100,000 years or more ago. But because of a misinterpretation of a specimen fossil back in 1911, for many decades afterward, the name "Neanderthaler" summoned up the image of a hairy, bowlegged brute who lumbered about grunting orders, wolfed down his food, and got the attention of his mate most often by grabbing her hair. In short, it was Neanderthal Man, long misunderstood, who gave us our enduring comic book vision of the early human cave dwellers.

In 1957, a reexamination of the fossil revolutionized our thinking about the Neanderthal population. The skeleton, it turned out, belonged to a man (estimated to be in his mid-forties at his death) who had suffered a severe arthritic disease of the joints. He may well have walked with a stooped gait, but this was because of his illness, not as was long supposed, because Neanderthalers couldn't walk like normal human beings! Later finds bore this out. Contrary to the opinion of an earlier day, we now think of the Neanderthalers as members of our own species, *Homo sapiens.* Certainly from the size of their skulls, there is reason to believe they were as smart as we are.

From what we can tell from their fossils, those Neanderthalers who lived in Europe had a very distinctive look. They had long faces, broad noses, and jaws that jutted forward quite noticeably. They were built like wrestlers, short and compact, and they had more powerful back muscles than are found anywhere among people living today.

They lived at a time when most of England and Ireland

What a Neanderthaler may have looked like. They could make fire and sew clothes; they buried their dead and had some idea of an afterlife. The legacy of the Neanderthalers is still with us.

was covered by a huge glacier, and for hundreds of miles to the south of those countries the weather was virtually subarctic. Only a few thousand people were living in Europe then, and they wisely took to systematically living in caves. Perhaps they covered the cave entries with hides to deflect the sometimes savage winds.

We know that the Neaderthalers were clever enough to make fires and also clothes to keep themselves warm. We even have the needles they used to sew them! They also made a wide variety of specialized stone implements which anthropologists refer to as the *Mousterian industry.* In addition to using the older type of hand axes, they invented a tool ideally suited to scraping, one that would have served well in the preparation of pelts.

Far more provocative are the remaining traces of the Neanderthalers' symbolic world. These are more difficult to decipher, for they depend on an intimate knowledge of those distant people's thinking, a realm we can never fully enter.

Even before Neanderthal times, people had begun to do something quite peculiar with animal skulls. For example, in France, at a cave called Lazaret, near Nice, the remains of three individuals were found (one of them a youth who apparently died of an infection). Nearby, wolf skulls were placed in a way that suggests that their presence and positioning held a special meaning for those who put them there.

The Neanderthalers continued—perhaps elaborated— this tradition. In a cave in southern Russia, for example, a teenager was buried surrounded by six goat skulls whose horns had been pushed into the ground. And at another burial in a cave at Regourdou in southern France a stone-lined pit was found to contain the upturned skulls of more than twenty bears. When alive, these animals, which are similar to the Alaskan brown bear, would have weighed three-quarters of a ton (0.7 metric ton) each and when standing erect would have been 10 feet (3 meters) tall.

The habit of burying certain individuals with skulls of wild and powerful animals seems therefore to have been a long-standing and widespread practice. What exactly the presence of these skulls symbolized to the cave dwellers is something we'll probably never know. But some burials

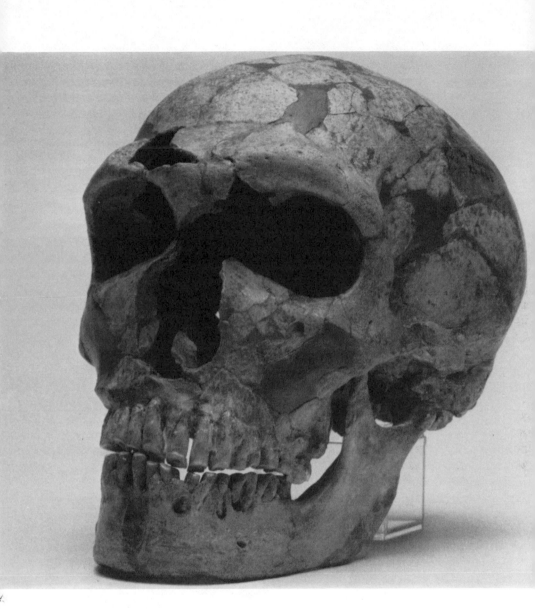

Neanderthal skull found in France.
Once thought to be too much of a dun-
derhead to be classed with ourselves,
Neanderthalers are now recognized
to be members of our own species.

Tools made by Stone Age people. Those numbered
5 to 7 were invented by the Neanderthalers.

found in the Middle East strongly suggest that people living at this time already had some conception of an afterlife.

In what is now modern Iraq, Israel, and Syria, tens of thousands of years before the civilizations of ancient Egypt and Mesopotamia, Neanderthalers were burying their rela- tives and friends along with gifts, the kind that would nourish and protect them on their way to the other world: a set of flint tools, for example, or a joint of cooked meat.

Significantly, many of the skeletons found in these burials don't have the "classic" western European Neander- thal look; they are taller, more slender, and in general seem more modern. Others combine traits of Neanderthal and modern populations. Clearly, the Middle East was a busy crossroads even in those early times.

The most recent Neanderthaler in western Europe clocked in about 35,000 years ago. Then for the next 10,000 years the fossil record there is maddeningly mute. Through- out this period the caves remained occupied, judging from the garbage that continued to accumulate in them, but as for the bones of the inhabitants themselves—nothing. The next ones to surface belong to people indistinguishable from liv- ing Europeans. The question that naturally arises is: what happened to the Neanderthalers?

The answer is that no one knows for sure.

An old and persistent view is that they represent a dead- end regional development. That is, they lived in Europe at the same time as the more modern-looking types who eventually replaced them, presumably with the aid of a superior technol- ogy. In a version that has been popularized by the media, the two groups fought it out with clubs and spears. The native Neanderthalers not only lost the conflict; their population was completely wiped out by the invaders. In this manner they disappeared from the face of the earth.

There hasn't exactly been a revolution in anthropolo- gists' thinking about the fate of the Neanderthalers, who in some way are so close to us, yet manage in the end to elude us. Perhaps this is because there have been no sensational fossil finds in recent years that would cause people to change their minds overnight.

There has, however, been an *evolution* of thought on this

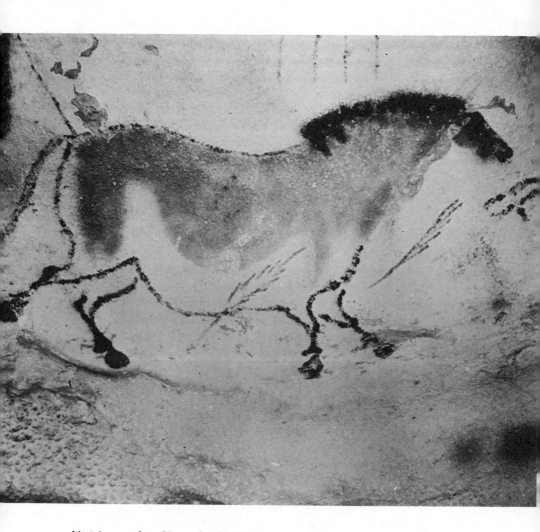

Not long after Neanderthal times, we find
the traces of wonderful paintings left for
us by Stone Age people in the far reaches of
the caves they once used. This painting from
the cave in France known as Lascaux is one
of a series of horses. Some are almost ten
feet long; others are quite small. In a
number of them, like this one, the animals
are depicted with arrows in their bodies.

question. That is, more and more anthropologists are leaning toward the view that the Neanderthalers neither disappeared nor became extinct. Instead, they believe, they simply evolved into the more modern-looking population we find living in Europe from 25,000 years ago and on. How could this be?

The hypothesis is that the climate and isolation caused by the glacier were responsible for the distinctive European Neanderthal build. (It does help people living in cold climates to have a low surface area/body mass ratio, because this prevents heat loss.) But because their isolation was never complete (recall the hybrids of the Middle East), the Europeans were able to reestablish contact with other groups whenever the weather permitted.

Surely not all of those renewed contacts were hostile. Mating must have taken place more often than maiming. According to today's thinking, the gene pool was where Neanderthalers and modern-looking humans met.

With the end of the Ice Age, the climatic pressure for the classic Neanderthal build was no longer present. Perhaps that is why their descendants resembled the newcomers, with whom they mated, more than themselves. In any case, while it's far from certain, anthropologists now suspect that the Neanderthalers, or rather their genes, are still with us.

CHAPTER 6
HE-MAN, SHE-MAN: SEX ROLES AND OUR ANCESTORS

*T*he *Australopithecus* seen repeatedly whacking the skull of a fellow hominid with a bone in the film *2001* was an adult male. To be faithful to the views of anthropology at that time, it had to be a male who invented the first tool, which of course was really a weapon. Males were the dominant sex.

With the discovery of how much more powerful they could be with this new invention in hand, they became the protectors of the females and the young. They went on to invent the spear and in time more sophisticated projectiles for bringing down their quarry. Triumphantly, they would return in a group with meat for the starving little ones and the womenfolk. The women, of course, would have had to stay behind to take care of the infants and young children.

Each hunter returned at the end of the day to a particular female. In exchange for "bringing home the bacon," he could expect a night of pure delight. For such an enticement, who wouldn't be willing to protect and provide for one of these vulnerable, powerless creatures and her dependents? Though perhaps unable to express them, such were the beliefs that animated the typical early hominid hunter as he trudged back from work at sunset. At least according to some anthropologists.

To others, almost everything in this picture is wrong. To them, the 1966 anthropological conference entitled "Man the Hunter" provided the most concrete evidence why.

Some of the participants still maintained the old view that hunting had dominated the human experience for hundreds of thousands of years. Hunting, they said, "made females and young dependent on male skills."* It produced our species' superior intellect. It was the reason we now are who we are.

But in fact what most of the papers showed was that the conference was really misnamed. It should have been called "Woman the Gatherer." Many of those present had gone to the far corners of the globe to study the lives of the last remaining hunters. They returned with the discovery that by and large it was the labor of the hunters' wives that put most of the food on the table.

MODERN HUNTERS

The study of living peoples, no matter how "primitive," gives us only an imperfect view of those who lived a million years ago. Quite apart from the fact that primitive peoples are like ourselves, the end product of that vast time span of experience, today's hunter/gatherers live in environments that are typically quite different from those exploited by our earliest forbears.

Today's hunters are confined to the most barren places of the world, those not yet seen as desirable by land-grabbing civilization. As a result, some of them may have an even harder time earning a living from the earth than the hunters of yesteryear.

Still, when taken as a whole, the studies made of living hunters by cultural anthropologists in the 1960s and 1970s have revolutionized much of our thinking about the culture of the earliest people. In particular, they have a lot to say about the sexual division of labor: what work men do versus what work women do. They show, for example, that while the

*See the article "The Evolution of Hunting" by Sherwood L. Washburn and C. S. Lancaster in *Man the Hunter*, edited by Richard Lee and Irven De Vore (Chicago: Aldine, 1968).

hunting activities of men are sporadic, the food-producing efforts of women are more regular.

Take the !Kung* Bushmen of the Kalahari Desert in Africa. Men often leave the group camp for a week or so to go in search of game. But for any of a number of reasons, including a run of bad luck, they may stop hunting altogether for a month or more. What do they do then? Richard Lee, a well-known ethnographer of the !Kung, says that "during these periods visiting, entertaining, and especially dancing are the primary activities of the men."†

What do the women do while the men are cavorting about? They are scanning the landscape for groceries. Kneeling on the parched earth, digging with the aid of simple, wooden sticks, they are uncovering any of thirty different varieties of roots and tubers. They are searching for the nests of wild bees for honey. They are picking the choicest of the twenty-nine species of fruits, berries, and melons that are available (when they're in season) to fling into their sacks. And always they are on the lookout for mondongo nuts. These are so tasty and nutritious that each Bushman eats about three hundred of them a day!

To be fair, the men and women put in roughly equal hours in search of food: two to three days of work per week per person (although these people themselves do not recognize a seven-day week). But it is the labor of the women which provides the bulk of the food eaten by everyone: by weight, two to three times the amount contributed by the men. Vegetable matter consists of a whopping 60 to 80 percent of the total Bushman diet. And it's a nutritionally significant contribution that the women make. The daily portion of mondongo nuts collected for one adult is equivalent in protein to 14 ounces (397 grams) of lean beef!

The Bushmen are not, at least today, an unusual case. It turns out that except in the Arctic, women in almost all modern hunting/gathering populations regularly contribute comparable percentages of their group's food.

---

*The exclamation point appearing before this group's name symbolizes a sound that doesn't exist in English, a click made way back in the throat.
†See "What Hunters Do for a Living, or How to Make Out on Scarce Resources," an article by Richard Lee in the book *Man the Hunter*.

*Getting the groceries in the Kalahari. This
!Kung woman is pounding the ground in search
of tubers with the aid of the traditional digging
stick. It's women's work that provides the
biggest portion of !Kung family meals.*

Consequently, some anthropologists have come to sus-pect that this was always so, except in the relatively rare (and recent) times when the Ice Age served up herds of large ani-mals but little in the way of plant food. Why hadn't we guessed this before? One reason is that animal bones leave more permanent, or at least more obvious traces than do the remains of eaten vegetal matter.

Most anthropologists now concede that hominid and ear-ly human females were undoubtedly providers, not just moochers. Nevertheless, some of them believe that the human revolution was a sexual revolution, and that it first began to snowball when males became more intent on cap-turing game.

THE HUMAN REVOLUTION: A THEORY

Between eight and fourteen million years ago in the days even before *Australopithecus*, the world experienced a change of climate. As a result, the lush tropical forests that had covered much of the Old World gradually began to shrink. Eventually in some places they were replaced by woodlands of less dense foliage and fewer edibles, and between them, savannahs: stretches of open grasslands dotted by even more sparsely scattered trees, a harsher landscape still.

Routed out of their treetop homes in the forest, the former primate tenants had to seek new lodgings, not to mention new sources of food. Those that had become highly specialized in their diet and could digest only certain kinds of leaves no doubt became extinct. Those with more omnivor-ous tastes (those who would eat almost anything) stood a better chance of adapting to the new environment.

For a long time it was assumed that our living primate cousins were strict vegetarians. But in the 1960s Jane Good-all corrected that wrong impression when she reported see-ing wild chimpanzees eating meat. Occasionally they actually joined forces to kill: usually an infant baboon or colobus mon-key left unattended. Other chimpanzee groups are now known to do the same, although meat constitutes only 1% of their diet. Dr. Goodall also reports that chimps sometimes walk on their hind legs for as much as thirty yards at a time when they carry things.

Using observations of chimpanzee behavior to speculate about our hominid ancestors is as tricky as using modern primitives as a time machine, for how can we be sure that *their* behavior hasn't changed over time, that what we are observing in the wild aren't new developments? Still, like two overlapping images that produce a three-dimensional stereo one, studies of primitive peoples and nonhuman primates together give us the impression of being able to reach out and touch something that isn't really there. In this case, it's the world of our distant ancestors.

If chimps dwelling in the abundant forest occasionally hunt small animals, and get up on their hind legs to carry food, then it seems likely that our hominid ancestors had mastered these skills by the time they ventured beyond the woodlands and out onto the African plains. But why did the hominids become real walkers whereas chimps and gorillas only resort to this form of locomotion for short distances?

According to the principle of natural selection, an organ, posture, or physical characteristic become part of a population's biology if by having it, individuals having it are better able to survive into the breeding age. The longer an animal lives, the more offspring it is likely to have. There's a good chance that these offspring will inherit the helpful trait and in their turn live longer, have more offspring, and pass it on to them, too. If the process goes on long enough, a once rare trait will eventually be found in most members of the population.

At first glance it would seem that on the savannah, being able to run on four legs like a baboon would be the best way of getting around. For one thing, it would ensure a swift getaway from dangerous animals (big meat-eating cats, for example). What possible greater survival advantage could walking on two have had for our ancestors?

The answer, according to anthropologists these days, is that it freed their hands, but not, as formerly thought, so they could make stone tools and weapons. That came millions of years later. The reason they needed their hands free was in order to carry things—specifically, tools, weapons, food and . . . babies. But why after millions of years did they suddenly need to carry these "things"? To understand, we have to look once again at where we were coming from.

EATING AND CARRYING AMONG CHIMPANZEES

In almost all nonhuman primate species, including the ground dwellers, individuals satisfy their own food needs. They do this mostly by foraging for fruits, insects, and seeds. The important exception observed so far is the occasional sharing of meat by chimps with those troop mates who continually "beg" for some with an outstretched hand, or who throw a tantrum if they don't get any! Jane Goodall reports one such case in which the chimp with meat finally relented, handing the beggar an entire hindquarter. Says Dr. Goodall: "It was as though he could no longer endure the screaming and commotion when he wanted to enjoy his prize."

Here meat is very much a treat. Because fruit is sufficiently abundant, these animals have no need to collect it and carry it back to a central location for storage or later distribution. So chimps don't need Tupperware or any of its historical precedents.

Nor do infants pose much of a carrying problem to the savannah ape or monkey mother. An infant is born with the reflex to cling to the fur of its mother's belly. Since the mother usually moves about on four legs, for the infant this means being carried upside down. But after five months the pattern changes and the mother hoists her youngster over her shoulder onto her back. Then he or she has to become an adept rider, and fairly quickly, too. Mother often travels at literally breakneck speed!

OUT OF THE FOREST

In the woodlands, where our hominid ancestors probably mastered walking, their hands were freed to carry sticks,

Chimps will not only occasionally kill game, but also share it with a troopmate. Here one chimp is "begging" for a piece of bushbuck by extending its hand with outstretched palm— a submissive gesture among chimps. The possessor of the meat seems to be giving the matter serious consideration.

Above and over: *at some point a baboon (and chimp) baby has to learn to cling to its parent's back rather than belly while being carried. Human babies often experience the same shift in positioning.*

stones and increasingly scarce foodstuffs back to an agreed upon location. But walking, coupled with the loss of fur, made the old primate mode of carrying infants no longer possible.

The use of a "Gerry-cuddler"—a sling that straps a baby chest to chest to an adult, a contraption increasingly being sported by American parents with newborns—probably comes closest to the basic primate mode of transporting the young. Quite possibly, one of its antecedents, an ancient "baby container" that has left no trace in the archeological record, was among the first human-invented tools.

If what we observe in forest-dwelling chimps today is any indication of how our joint common ancestor behaved, the "human revolution" was largely a changed relationship between youngsters and mature males.

Adult male chimpanzees are protective toward the young of their group, but for the most part only in a very general sort of way. They don't usually share food with the young, nor do they typically develop emotional attachments to particular youngsters (though exceptions have been observed). The mother/offspring bond, on the other hand, is very strong. Dr. Goodall reports examples of fully mature sons and daughters keeping in regular touch with their aging chimp mothers.

Some anthropologists feel that when our ancestors moved out into the less abundant woodlands and the savannah beyond, their survival chances were given a boon by a brand-new development: mature males helping mothers to raise their babies.

Hominid babies were being born smaller and more immature than before because with the establishment of upright posture, the female birth canal was reduced in size. These hominid females had to deliver earlier than their predecessors so that the baby could slip through the birth canal. But this meant that babies were helpless that much longer.

Anthropologist Owen Lovejoy suggests that adult males could have been particularly helpful at this time by bringing back food for the youngsters. At the very least, he says, these males probably exploited somewhat different areas for their own food so as not to compete with mothers and their young. But what induced males who were so long used to foraging with only themselves in mind to change their ways?

"More sex," is the answer given by some anthropologists.

Again, if today's primates are any clue to the past, our joint ancestor had a somewhat different reproductive system than that of human females. Conception, and in fact even intercourse, could only take place during the female's period of heat. (This lasts about fourteen days of the monthly menstrual cycle among chimps.) For the rest of the time, males and females would not have been sexually aroused by each other.

At some point, of course, all that changed. The questions have always been when, and under what circumstances? These are sticky questions because in this case the fossils are of no help to us at all. But recently, anthropologist Helen Fisher has put forward a hypothesis to explain how our human sexuality might have evolved. It is this:

In the new food-scarce environment in which our ancestors found themselves, females needed more food than before in order to nurture their tinier, more immature babies. Those hominid females who were sexually active for longer periods of time than was usual stood a better chance of attracting males to them. These males would probably share with them food which they had found or captured during the day. (And in fact Dr. Goodall has found that male chimps who have meat are more likely to share it with sexually active females than with others.)

Being better nourished as a result of these gifts of meat and being better protected, female hominids with longer periods of monthly sexual activity would have survived better and left more daughters who might well have inherited the same tendency. Eventually, with enough time, this process would lead to a population which like ourselves had a physical capacity for sex all month long. An increased capacity for sex, the habit of forming pair bonds (that is, close and enduring relationships between one male and one female), and a greater degree of parenting behavior assumed by mature males are all believed to have developed together; each pattern reinforced the others.

At the heart of the new complex of behaviors was the regular sharing of food. And if modern hunting peoples give us any clue to the past, the food contributions made by hominid females to their group was probably substantial. Sharing by both sexes was what spelled the survival of the hominids in the distant days when they were being transformed into human beings. Little wonder then that the communal enjoyment of food is still a cornerstone of all known cultures. Whenever we share food with others, we not only relish it more, we unconsciously celebrate a prime cause of our humanity.

CHAPTER 7

FEASTS AND FAMINE IN EARLY MEXICO: THE AZTEC CANNIBALISM CONTROVERSY

> . . . we found wooden cages made of lattice-work in which men and women were imprisoned and fed until they were fat enough to be sacrificed and eaten. . . . From now on, whenever we entered a town our captain's first order was to break down the cages and release the prisoners, for these prison cages existed throughout the country.

It sounds like it could be a scene in a new Indiana Jones movie, but it isn't. These words were written by Bernal Díaz, who was born in Spain in 1492, the same year that Columbus set sail for the East and discovered the West. When he was 84, Díaz took up his pen to describe what he had seen in his younger days as a member of the famous expedition under Hernando Cortés, which in the year 1519 led to the Spanish Conquest of Mexico.

Díaz claimed that he wanted to "describe plainly, as an honest witness" the events of the Conquest, and indeed it is the dry, usually undramatic tone of his narrative that is so compelling. Apart from that, much of what he reports is also to be found in the writings of the other Spanish chroniclers of those times.

Even in the small towns, the expedition regularly came upon the evidence of recent human sacrifice: temples awash with fresh blood and the stench of decaying corpses still hanging in the air. The Spanish conquistadors, themselves rather ferocious fighters, must have been anything but squeamish fellows. Still, the gory sights that Mexico presented "amazed" them, to use Díaz' word.

Eventually, they were forced to witness acts of sacrifice, not just the mess that remained afterward. Says Díaz: "Every day they sacrificed before our eyes three, four, or five Indians whose hearts were offered to the idols and whose blood was plastered to the walls."

At the "cues," or pyramid-shaped temples, the victims were marched up the steps (as many as 120 of them in the biggest cities) and had their still beating hearts torn out of them by the priests. Díaz describes how in the Aztec capital of Tenotchtitlán

a little apart from the "cue" stood another smaller tower . . . one of its doors was in the shape of a terrible mouth. This mouth was open and contained great fangs to devour souls. Beside this door were groups of devils and the shapes of serpents, and a little way off was a place of sacrifice, all blood-stained and black with smoke. There were many great pots and jars and pitchers in the house full of water. For it was here they cooked the flesh of those who were sacrificed and eaten by the papas (priests).*

Throughout their journey to the capital, according to Díaz, the little army tried to convince the local chiefs to put an end to this particular form of carnage. Cortés himself made impassioned speeches advising the Indians how much better it would be to destroy the temple idols, replace their dragons with a nice Christian cross and statue of the gentle Madonna, and to cease eating, if not killing, their neighbors. But his pleadings were said to be in vain.

*See The Conquest of New Spain, written by Bernal Díaz and translated by J. M. Cohen (New York: Penguin Books, 1963).

Kick out the old idols? Who would bring the rain, the crops, good health? the chiefs wanted to know. The Madonna might provide for the Spanish, but would she do the same for the people of Mexico?

Who were the victims of sacrifice? Much of what little we know on this subject comes from the writings of Bernardo de Sahagún, a friar who arrived on the scene from Spain ten years after Mexico fell to the Spanish. He was, in a way, a very early anthropologist, for he took the trouble to learn the Aztec language and he systematically questioned the surviving Indians about their culture. Eventually, the information he gathered in this manner filled thirteen volumes which are known as *The Florentine Codex*. From it we learn that the sacrificial victims were mostly prisoners of war.

The Aztec army was huge. It could capture thousands of prisoners in a single battle. The Spanish were told that in 1487, for example, the dedication of a new temple was celebrated by having four lines of prisoners of war stretching for two miles sacrificed by executioners working nonstop for four days and nights: a total of fourteen thousand people killed for one event!

It would be easy to dismiss this as mere boasting or an attempt on the part of the Indians to frighten off the small army of Spanish intruders, were it not for the words of Bernal Díaz. In the plaza of Xocotlan, he says, "there were piles of human skulls so regularly arranged that one could count them, and I estimated there were more than a hundred thousand. I repeat again there were more than a hundred thousand of them." And he was not one to repeat himself.

Recently, two anthropologists, Michael Harner and Marvin Harris, have—using Díaz, Sahagún, and other early chroniclers as their guides—taken a close look at the place of sacrifice and cannibalism in the culture of sixteenth century Mexico. They believe that both were practiced on a grand scale and for the reason that they provided protein for a portion of the population.*

*Michael Harner's theory is spelled out in his article "The Ecological Basis for Aztec Cannibalism" in *American Ethnologist*, vol. 4, no. 1, Feb. 1977. Marvin Harris elaborates on the theory in his book *Cannibals and Kings* in the chapter entitled "The Cannibal Kingdom" (NY: Random House, 1977).

*An early Mexican codex
showing a temple sacrifice*

While their theory has not exactly revolutionized thinking about Aztec culture—at least in the sense of toppling older views of it—it has sparked a major controversy among anthropologists. It is possible that in the end our understanding not only of the Aztecs, but of ourselves as well, will be forever altered by the debate.

CULTURAL MATERIALISM

The approach used by Harner and Harris is called *cultural materialism* and it is one that *did* revolutionize anthropology in the 1960s. Essentially it is a type of analysis that tries to explain cultural habits—including those that on the surface seem quite bizarre or irrational—in terms of very basic, practical needs: the needs of a population to feed itself, for example. This may sound simple, but establishing the connection between the two is often not such an easy matter.

Recently, cultural materialist analyses have been used to explain such different patterns of behavior as the ancient Hebrew prohibition against eating pork and the habit of some New Guinea tribes to "pig out" on the stuff as part of *their* religious ceremonies. In order to understand why particular practices such as these two opposite ones developed, we first need to know certain things. In particular, we need to know something of the *ecology* of the particular place where the practice in question began: that is, the relationship between its plants, animals, and human inhabitants.

THE ECOLOGY OF MEXICO

Like most parts of the world after the last Ice Age, Mexico was left with a depleted supply of animals. In fact, it was left more impoverished than other places. But somehow people there managed to survive, and some time before 800 B.C. they discovered how to grow corn and beans and other edible plants.

In time, these foods allowed the early Mexicans to expand their populations and to become *civilized*, as anthropologists use the term. That is, peoples like the Mayans had enough surplus food and time on their hands to build such things as major irrigation works, temples that may well have served as astronomical observatories, and impressive government complexes. The Mayans were a literate people. Their books were made of paper manufactured from the bark of the fig tree. Their system of writing was a sophisticated one that combined pictorial signs representing whole words and phonetic signs representing sounds.

But some time after 800 A.D., the Mayan civilization suddenly collapsed. One theory is that it had been built upon an ecological base that was so fragile that a number of factors could at any time have brought about its destruction: erosion of soil, build-up of silt in the canals, and deforestation which causes changes in the pattern of annual rainfall.

Water was life, and beginning about 1100 A.D. the people living in the Valley of Mexico began work on a vast new irrigation project. They built a network of drainage ditches along the margin of a large shallow lake. As a result of their labors, the entire area soon became enormously productive, and within a few centuries the regional population had swelled to two million.

Tenochtitlán, the seat of Emperor Montezuma's power, was strategically located on an island connected to the lake's shore by one of the three causeways the Indians had built. Cortés and his men were familiar with the cities of Spain and with Rome and Constantinople, too, but they were nonetheless "astounded" at their first glimpse of the Aztec capital: ". . . buildings rising from the water, all made of stone, seemed like an enchanted vision . . . Indeed, some of our soldiers asked whether it was not all a dream."

Bernal Díaz goes on to describe at length the city on the lake with its flat-roofed houses accessible to one another only by canoe or wooden drawbridge. It was a city as lively and lovely and wonderfully improbable as Venice.

There were courts paved with smooth white flagstones and shrines that "looked like gleaming white towers and castles." There were palaces with orchards and gardens where "everything was shining with lime." And the market was a world unto itself, bustling as a Middle Eastern bazaar.

There were stalls for the dealers of silver, gold, and pre-

Tikal, Mexico. The early Mexicans built great ceremonial centers. They were a combination of government complex, temples, and sports stadia and possibly included an astronomical observatory.

cious stones, for the vendors of feathers, fabrics, and embroidered goods. Others sold tools, timber, tobacco, or pottery. There were greengrocers, herbalists, chocolate and nougat merchants, people who sold prepared foods, and others who sold live rabbits, ducks, birds, and dogs.

In short, the Spaniards gazed upon a panorama of plenty. But according to Harner and Harris, it was a mirage. They believe that ecological overload had again been reached; there were simply too many people competing for too little available protein. For by this time only the upper classes of Tenochtitlán could afford to eat such luxuries as rabbit, duck, turkey, fish, and dog.

Ordinary people had to content themselves with beans, maize-cakes (corn kneaded with eggs), and *tecuitlatl*, meaning "stone dung." This was something people made from a substance they skimmed off the surface of the lake as it floated by. It was a kind of weed, according to Bernal Díaz, which curdled and tasted a bit like cheese but was made into small (and apparently hard, judging from the name) cakelike patties. People also ate the spongy nests of water-fly larvae.

Corn and beans, says Harner, might have provided the poorer people with necessary protein, but only if consumed in large quantities on a regular basis. Unfortunately, there were years when crops failed and famine was a real threat.

Twice in Montezuma's reign there had been serious food shortages. And in fact the Aztec ruler repeatedly tried to dissuade the Spaniards from entering his city by sending Cortés this message: Don't come. There's not enough food for you here! The army, by then numbering only about 400, paid no heed and pressed on toward the capital.

When at last the Spaniards arrived at the palace of the great prince, they were (at least at first) received as honored guests and so had the opportunity to view at close range the life-styles of the rich and famous.

For each meal the servants prepared more than thirty different dishes. Fowls, turkeys, pheasants, partridges, quail, duck, venison, boar, hares, and pigeons were featured main courses. One more thing, according to Bernal Díaz: the flesh of young boys.

But there were things that were always missing from Montezuma's dinner table: items such as beef, pork, lamb, goat. Why?

According to Harner and Harris, the answer is the key to understanding why the Aztec gods demanded human hearts and blood whereas those of the Middle East were content with offerings of goats and wine. The reason, they say, is that these animals did not exist in Mexico. Nor were there any other native herbivores (plant-feeding mammals) to take their place in people's diets. No cows and no goats not only meant there was no meat from these animals, but no milk, butter, cheese, or yogurt.

In Mexico, the increasing frequency of food shortages coincided with a rise in the gods' demand for human sacrifice. But the deities required only the victims' hearts and blood. That left their trunks, limbs, and fleshy parts as food for certain sectors of the population. And who got to dine on these?

According to Harris, it wasn't only the very wealthy like Montezuma and his friends (who could also afford alternative sources of meat), but the far less well-to-do and peasant soldiers who captured the sacrificed prisoners in enemy territory. For them, a free meat meal of any sort would have been welcomed. What it represented was a kind of "bonus pay" aimed at ensuring their continued loyalty to their ruler.

THE CRITICS RESPOND

The critics of this theory are themselves divided on what they disagree about. One camp denies the existence of protein deficiency in sixteenth century Mexico and claims that cannibalism was not necessary. The other denies the existence of cannibalism altogether.

According to Bernardo Montellano, before the Spanish conquered Mexico its inhabitants cultivated amaranth, a staple grain that was high in protein. In addition, he says, they had the nutritional benefit of numerous wild and domesticated vegetables. A meatless diet isn't necessarily devoid of protein.

Along similar lines, anthropologist Barbara Price argues

that the Spanish introduction of domestic animals such as cows, pigs, and goats into Mexico has done little to alter the diet of the bulk of that country's population: that is, its poor people. Today's peasants, like their sixteenth century Indian counterparts, can afford to eat meat only rarely. Meat is a luxury item reserved for the celebration of important occasions. For the most part, ordinary people get their protein from large quantities of corn and beans.

Dr. Price thinks it's wrong to think of the Aztecs going off to war for the purpose of capturing enemy prisoners to feed people who would have no protein otherwise. But she does agree that the meat of cannibalized victims was a luxury item used by members of the wealthier classes to appease potential troublemakers. In other words, she imagines the corpses of the victims being used in the way we're always seeing bottles of fancy liquor used in wartime movies, that is, to woo people into the service of the powerful.

The most dramatic blow to the Harner theory comes from W. Arens, who denies not only the existence of protein deficiency in sixteenth century Mexico, but the existence of cannibalism as well! It was, he claims, a necessary fiction from the very beginning.

Dr. Arens points out that none of the long letters written by Cortés from the field during the Conquest makes any mention of it. Only years later, when the Mexican Indians and their culture had been all but wiped out by the Spanish, did the first memoirs of the participants, with their frequent allusions to cannibalism, come to be written. He says: "By then they were different men, living in different times. The consequences of the Conquest were becoming a matter of some moral concern, and the fate of the Indians, too. . . ."

In other words, the Spanish were trying to justify their near destruction of the native Mexican population by making the Indians appear to be abhorrent and inhuman. As Dr. Arens rightly, points out: despite all Bernal Díaz' allusions, Díaz never describes ever actually witnessing people eating other people. He assumes a great deal. The great skull racks, for example, do not by themselves tell us, or Díaz, the fate of their owners.

In the years after the Conquest, the main job of the Spanish friars sent to Mexico was to convert the surviving Indians to Christianity. This was a task that had to have colored the writings of those, like Sahagún, who took a genuine scholarly interest in the Indians' culture. Their "ethnographies" were often scrutinized by religious offices. To justify conversion, it was important, Dr. Arens argues, to establish a huge gulf to lay between Christians and "pagans," and the taste for human flesh clearly filled the bill.

As his deathblow to the "cannibalism for food" theory, he cites the situation in the capital after the Spanish seized it. By then the inhabitants of Tenochtitlán were suffering terribly. One of Sahagún's Aztec informants in recalling those days said the survivors ate anything: "they ate colorin wood and they ate glue orchid, and the frilled flower and tanned hides, and buckskin which they roasted, baked, toasted or burned, so that they could eat them; and they gnawed sedum [a flowering plant] and mud brick."

But there is no mention of eating the bodies of the dead that were piled all around. Nor do the memoirs of the few Aztecs who, like Díaz, felt the need to tell the story of their times make mention of cannibalism. This is most peculiar, for these Indians freely admitted that captured Spaniards were sacrificed; there is simply no mention of anyone dining on their limbs. Where then does the truth of the matter lay?

NO EASY ANSWER

As with many questions posed by anthropologists, the answers are probably far less simple than at first was supposed. Only in time will we have the full answers, and then most likely due to the exposure of untruths, the invariable consequence of controversy.

Does it matter in the end whether the Aztecs cannibalized their victims five centuries ago, and if they did so, does it matter whether the practice stemmed from a nutritional need? How do the alternative answers affect our view of humankind, and of our own society's situation today?

If the answers to the first two questions are yes—that is, that the Aztecs indeed cannibalized their neighbors to a startling degree and out of nutritional need—then the cultural materialist explanation of their culture has a special relevance for our own. If the answers are yes, then ecological factors were at work in sixteenth century Mexico that eventually may have caused the collapse of that civilization even if Europeans had never crossed the Atlantic. But this is not to say that it would not have revived. Perhaps in time, native Mexicans would have again created new energy-saving systems that would have sparked renewed population growth and brought about an improved standard of living.

A cultural materialist view of history is one that looks toward ecology and economics for explanations of cultural beliefs and practices. It looks for relationships between the use of new technologies, population booms, the material improvement of life, and the collapse of civilization. If it is true, as some people today feel, that we are on the cusp of self-destruction, we might well look to the Aztecs. Not because any one sector of our society is in danger of being eaten by another—at least literally—but because, in the words of Marvin Harris:

> what is happening to today's standard of living has happened in the past. Our culture is not the first technology that has failed. Nor is it the first to reach its limits of growth. The technologies of earlier cultures failed again and again, only to be replaced by new technologies. And limits of growth have been reached and transcended only to be reached and transcended again.

If, on the other hand, the answer to the first two questions raised is "no, the Aztecs never ate one another, or even their enemies," that, too has great relevance for us. Because if that should be true, it means that some Europeans and Americans (including contemporary anthropologists) have long accepted a myth about the Indians as historical fact. If, as Dr. Arens claims, that myth was created by Europeans of the time to justify the conquest and colonization of Mexico, we had better take heed. It serves to warn us how enduring cultural slander can be, and how far social science can wander from its ideal of complete objectivity. If true, it shows that ultimately social scientists are first and foremost members of their own society. Unfortunately, despite their very best efforts to be free of their society's values—at least while they are at work—sometimes anthropologists are unconscious heirs to that society's historic blind spots.

CHAPTER 8
NEW DIRECTIONS
FOR ANTHROPOLOGY

CULTURE CHANGE

Forty years ago if anyone saw a movie that showed "primitives," chances were it was a Tarzan film. Usually in these films the primitives were a horde of nameless, spear-throwing Africans, although occasionally the native inhabitants might be seen in the role of porters to white adventurers.

Compare that with the situation today. In two of 1985's popular commercial films, "primitives" are the main characters, not just hundreds of extras used to create scenery. And it is the plight of the primitive in our fast-changing world that is, in both cases, the main story.

The Gods Must Be Crazy tells what happens when a Coke bottle—that universal symbol of modern Western civilization and its encroachment everywhere—suddenly lands amidst a group of people whom we have met before: Bushmen of the Kalahari Desert. The empty bottle creates havoc among them, for although the people soon discover that while it makes an excellent, all-purpose tool, it is unfortunately a one-of-a-kind commodity (unique in this respect among them) and therefore extremely difficult to share. Sharing resources is at the very heart of hunting/gathering culture, and it is this custom which the (at first) seemingly wonderful Coke bottle soon threatens to destroy. Because they have sent the people such a dangerous gift, the gods must be crazy.

That at least some Bushmen are performing in a movie is a testament to how far they have come from the completely isolated kind of people whom they are playing in it. This does not mean that they are professional actors who are as far from the traditional Bushman life style depicted in the film as we are. But it is a fact that most Bushmen who hunted and gathered for their livelihood as recently as the 1960s no longer do so.

Today they are more likely to work as hired hands for neighboring farming peoples. As a result, they now drive trucks and are familiar with much modern technology. For the Bushmen, the hunting/foraging way of life is becoming extinct.

That is also true for those who dwell in the rain forests of Brazil, the setting of *The Emerald Forest.* Using the story of a white father's search through the Amazon for his long-kidnapped son as its point of departure, this film is very much about the present predicament of the Indians of the region. Their culture, as well as the great forest which is their home, is in danger of being destroyed by the vast, engulfing construction projects that modern society has masterminded and set into motion in the Amazon.

More than forty years ago, the great French anthropologist Claude Lévi-Strauss stalked these very same jungles in search not of a missing son, but rather the last remaining Indians known not to have had contact with the modern world. At the time there was a real fear among some anthropologists that once the last primitives had been observed and written about, they themselves must forever close their notebooks, and like the people who were once the objects of their research, consult the classifieds for other kinds of work.

That fear has not prevailed. "Culture change" itself has recently become a major target of anthropological study.

What happens when peoples like the Bushmen or the Indians of the Amazon migrate to cities, or enter the modern labor market? What happens not only to them as individuals, but to their shared patterns of marriage and kinship, their

At home in the tent of an African family.
The girl on the right is shaking milk in an
inflated goatskin to make butter. But it would
be wrong to think of her and her family as be-
ing unconnected to the modern world. Why?

political ties and religious beliefs? How are the bits and pieces of two such completely different ways of life fused into a whole? And how is this new whole transmitted to the next generation? Or is it? Finding the answers to these and similar questions is the job of many of today's cultural anthropologists. Those who document what happens to transplanted people and their traditional cultures in cities practice what is now called "urban anthropology."

Some do more than just document the often grim facts about people whose homelands have been taken over by modern society. They represent these people and work toward helping them to win cases against governments and corporations. They also work in government, business, industry, and social services, providing anthropological data and perspectives so that people can better understand one another. These are relatively new roles for anthropologists. Those who are engaged in these kinds of applied research outside of academic institutions call themselves "practicing anthropologists."

It should also be said that today's anthropologists are to be found not only in exotic, out-of-the-way corners of the world, or in its teeming cities. They may also be encountered in suburban malls or parks, and not necessarily as unemployed idlers. What, you may well ask, are they doing here? One possibility is that they are studying cultural patterns in the way people use space, an area of research known as *proxemics.*

PROXEMICS

This is a field whose importance is just coming to be appreciated by firms that do much of their business in foreign countries. As it turns out, even the apparently simple matter of facing a person you wish to converse with involves rules that vary from one part of the globe to another. Ordinarily, no one bothers to talk about these rules because they are learned in early childhood and therefore seem to us not to be learned at all, just intuitive wisdom about how to behave in perfectly natural ways.

Anthropologist Edward Hall discovered, for example, that the habit Americans have of strolling with eyes facing

Cultures vary in the amount of distance they prescribe for people engaged in conversation. In Morocco, for example, eyeball-to-eyeball contact is normal for casual conversation.

forward and only occasionally glancing at the person with whom they are at the same time conversing is regarded as thoroughly erratic and impolite behavior by Arabs. To them, "correct" behavior requires you to be face-to-face all the while you are talking to someone.

Furthermore, Americans and Arabs have a different sense of what the proper distance is between two people having a conversation. When circumstances throw unknowing people from two such different cultures together, they can often be seen doing an awkward little dance as each person tries to compensate for the constantly changing "proper" distance created by the movement of the other.

Gestures, postures, seating positions, and other uses of public space vary a good deal from one society to another, and these communicate—sometimes miscommunicate—information and attitudes without the use of verbal language. Some anthropologists are trying to create proxemic grammars; that is, they are trying to codify the culturally varying rules of this language without words.

TECHNOLOGY

We've already mentioned the impact of modern technology on the lives of former "primitives." But recent revolutions in technology have also affected anthropologists and the work they do.

Computers, of course, extend the frontiers of anthropological research by as yet unfathomed measures, as they do with all fields of systematic inquiry. They allow primatologists and cultural anthropologists to record and store unprecedented quantities of data on their respective animal and human subjects. They also aid archeologists in dramatic ways.

For example, computerized robot systems now permit the exploration of shipwrecks buried in previously inaccessible waters. Shipwrecks are virtual time capsules, for they contain not only maritime artifacts, but those that speak of the more mundane aspects of life in other times and places. In 1985, the long-sought "Titanic" was discovered, and just such a robot system was used to learn the contents of the famous wreck.

In the same year, computerized photogrammetry became available to archeologists. This photographic system enables them to summon at the press of a button a three-dimensional image of a building or part of a site that has had to be destroyed in order for further excavation of what lay beneath to proceed. At the same time, the precise measurements of all the artifacts appearing in the image are presented.

Space-Age technology is at the service of archeologists in other ways, too. Take, for example, the Mayan-built irrigation works we spoke of in the last chapter. Their existence was verified as recently as 1978, when a team of archeologists surveyed the Mexican lowland swamps from the air using radar developed by NASA for exploring the surface of Venus.

The machinery now at the disposal of anthropologists is indeed impressive. Yet despite a changed world and the presence of their newly acquired, often expensive technical baggage, anthropologists are still striving to fulfill the goals they have long held in common: to observe and record how we as a species are faring in the various circumstances we find ourselves; to explain our similarities and differences; and finally, to understand how we used culture—our great capacity for learning—to outwit the odds against our survival in the past.

Perhaps when fully realized, this last will be the longed-for key, not only to self-knowledge, but to our survival into the future.

GLOSSARY

Acheulian industry: the stone tools associated with *Homo erectus*

Archeology: the study of prehistoric and historic cultures through the analysis of material remains

Artifact: any human-made object

Australopithecus: an extinct genus of hominid; three species are recognized: *Australopithecus afarensis, Australopithecus africanus,* and *Australopithecus robustus.*

Australopithecines: plural of *Australopithecus*

Bipedal: walking on two legs

Civilization: a population characterized by a high level of political organization

Coprolite: fossilized excrement

Cranial capacity: the volume of the skull measured in cubic centimeters

Cultural anthropology: the study of cultural variation

Cultural materialism: a type of analysis that looks toward ecology and economics for explanations of cultural beliefs and practices

Culture: the set of learned values, behaviors, and beliefs shared by a particular population

Endocranial cast: any material that has solidified inside a skull so that it has taken on the shape of the braincase

Ethnography: a description of a population's customary behaviors, beliefs, and interactions with its neighbors and its environment

Ethnology: comparative and interpretative research in cultural anthropology

Foramen magnum: the hole at the base of the skull through which the spinal cord passes to ascend into the brain

Fossils: remains of organisms from past ages

Genealogy: an account of the ancestry of a particular person or family

Genus: a group of related species

Grammar: a set of rules explaining how to combine the units of a language into meaningful words and sentences

Half-life: the time it takes for half of one isotope to become another through radioactive decay

Hominid: relating to the human family, which includes all forms of *Australopithecus* and *Homo*

Homo: the genus to which human beings belong

Homo erectus: an extinct species of our genus which lived in Java, China, Africa, and Europe for one million years

Homo habilis: a term applied to certain hominid fossils from East Africa that are believed by some to be a distinct species of Homo

Homo sapiens: the human species

Mousterian industry: the use of stone tools associated with the Neanderthalers; it is basically a flake industry with its predominant tool being the scraper

Neanderthalers: a subgrouping of the modern human species that lived between 35,000 and 100,000 years ago

Neolithic: a prehistoric period extending from the beginnings of agriculture in the Middle East to the introduction of metalworking

Order: a category of related zoological families

Paleoanthropologists: those physical anthropologists concerned with the time period in which hominids were emerging from earlier primate stock

Piltdown Man: a hominid "fossil" discovered in England in 1912 and proven to be a hoax

Pithecanthropus erectus: the name originally given to the earliest discovered specimens of *Homo erectus*

Potassium-argon dating: a method of dating certain volcanic rock by measuring the amount of argon that has been formed in the period since the rock was molten

Primates: the order of mammals to which humans, monkeys, lorises, apes, lemurs, and tarsiers belong

Primatologists: those physical anthropologists who study the biology and behaviors of nonhuman primates

Protoculture: those sets of behaviors observed in nonhuman primates that are both learned and distinctive to particular troops

Proxemics: the study of cultural differences in people's use of space

Sociobiology: a controversial school of thinking which proposes a genetic basis for much of human behavior

Species: a group of closely related organisms which if living in the same time and place have the ability to reproduce fertile offspring

Stereoscopic vision: the ability to see in three dimensions

Taboo: a cultural prohibition which if violated is often believed to bring about supernatural punishment

BIBLIOGRAPHY

Benedict, Ruth. *Patterns of Culture*. Boston: Houghton Mifflin, 1934.

Boas, Franz. *Race, Language, and Culture*. New York: Macmillan, 1940.

Chagnon, Napoleon A. *Yanomamao: The Fierce People*. New York: Holt, Rinehart, and Winston, 1968.

Darwin, Charles. *The Origins of Species*. London: John Murray, 1859.

DuBois, Cora. *The People of Alor*. Minneapolis: The University of Minnesota Press, 1944.

Fisher, Elizabeth. *Woman's Creation: Sexual Evolution and the Shaping of Society*. New York: McGraw Hill, 1979.

Fisher, Helen. *The Sex Contract*. New York: William Morrow & Company, 1982.

Frazer, Sir James George. *The Golden Bough: A Study in Magic and Religion*. N.Y.: Criterion Books. Abridged in one volume: The Macmillan Company paperback edition, 1963.

Fox, Robin. *Kinship and Marriage: An Anthropological Perspective*. Baltimore: Penguin, 1967.

Fried, Morton. *The Study of Anthropology*. New York: Thomas Y. Crowell, 1972.

Friedl, Ernestine. *Vasilika: A Village in Modern Greece*. New York: Holt, Rinehart and Winston, 1962.

Hall, Edward T. *The Hidden Dimension*. New York: Doubleday, 1969.

Hayes, Cathy. *The Ape in Our House*. New York: Harper & Row, 1951.

Hays, H.R. *From Ape to Angel: An informal history of social anthropology*. New York: Capricorn Books, 1958.

Kardiner, Abram and Edward Preble. *They Studied Man*. Toronto: New American Library, 1963.

Leakey, Richard. *The Making of Mankind*. New York: E.P. Dutton, 1981.

Lévi-Strauss, Claude. *Tristes Tropiques*. New York: Atheneum, 1967.

Lewis, Oscar. *La Vida: A Puerto Rican Family in the Culture of Poverty—San Juan and New York*. New York: Random House, 1965.

Malinowski, Bronislaw. *Magic, Science, and Religion & Other Essays*. Garden City, New York: Doubleday, 1954.

_____. *Argonauts of the Western Pacific*. New York: E. P. Dutton, 1961. Originally published 1944.

Mead, Margaret. *Coming of Age in Samoa*. New York: William Morrow, 1928.

_____. *Growing Up in New Guinea*. New York: William Morrow, 1930.

_____. *Letters from the Field: 1925-1975*. New York: Harper & Row, 1977.

Turnbull, Colin. *The Forest People*. New York: Simon & Schuster, 1961.

Whorf, Benjamin Lee. *Language, Thought and Reality*. John B. Carroll, ed. New York: John Wiley & Sons, 1956.

INDEX

Acheulian industry, 69–70
Africa
    exploration for hominids, 48–57
    see also Hominids
Aggression, heredity and, 15
Altruism, 15
Animals, naming of, 34–35
Anthropological linguistics, 27–29
    goal of, 29
Anthropology
    anthropological linguistics, 27–29
    archeology, 26–27
    computers, use in, 114–115
    cultural anthropology, 29–31
    cultural materialism, 99, 106
    culture change, study of, 110, 112
    goals of study, 10–11
    physical anthropology, 17–25
    proxemics, 112, 114
    urban anthropology, 112
Apes. *See* Primate studies
Archeology, 26–27
    goals of, 26–27
    neolithic era, study of, 26–27
    "new archeology," 27
Arens, W., 104, 106
Artifacts, 26
Australopithecus, 49–50, 52, 53–57

!Kung Bushmen, study of,
83

Language
   anthropological linguis-
      tics, 27–29
   grammar, 29
   social position and use
      of, 27–28
   see also Primate lan-
      guage learning
Leakey, Louis, 40, 55, 57
Leakey, Mary, 55, 57, 64
Leakey, Richard, 58
Learning, transmission over
   generations, 37–38
Lee, Richard, 83
Levi–Strauss, Claude, 110
Lovejoy, Owen, 92
Lucy, 58, 60, 64
   characteristics of, 60
   erect walking, 60, 64
Lunchtime, origin of, 23

Macaca fuscata. See Ma-
   caques
Macaques, 34–38
   culture of, 38
   foods given to, 35
   potato washing, 35, 37–
      38
Mating, definition of, 34–35
Mexico
   ecology of, 99–103
   food shortage of, 102–
      103
Missing link, 48, 67
Monkeys. *See* Primate studies

Montellano, Bernardo, 103
Mousterian industry, 74

Naming of animals, 34–35
   genus, 35
   species, 35–36
Natural selection, theory of,
   86
Neanderthaler, 72, 74, 77,
   79
   burial customs, 74, 77
   characteristics of, 72
   climate and, 79
   extinction of, 77, 79
   Mousterian industry
      and, 74
Neolithic era, study of, 26–
   27

Order, definition of, 19

Paleoanthropology, 22
Patterson, Francine, 43
Physical anthropology, 17–
   25
   paleoanthropology, 22
   primate studies, 18–19,
      22–23
   time span studied, 18
Pithecanthropus erectus, 67,
   68
   see also Homo erectus
Potassium argon method,
   57–58
   half–life in, 57–58
   sensitivity of, 60
Potato washing, macaques,
   35, 37–38
Price, Barbara, 103–104

ABOUT THE AUTHOR

A native New Yorker, Maxine Fisher received her B.A. from Queens College in 1968 and her Ph.D. in anthropology from the City University of New York Graduate Center in 1978. Her ethnographic research on the immigrants who came to the United States from India beginning in the late 1960s resulted in the publication of *The Indians of New York City*. Dr. Fisher currently teaches in the Department of Sociology and Anthropology at Bernard Baruch College of the City University of New York. She has written the screenplays for a number of short films. This is her first book for Franklin Watts.